God's Theatr

T. J. GORRINGE

God's Theatre

A Theology of Providence

SCM PRESS
London

First published 1991

SCM Press
26-30 Tottenham Road
London N1 4BZ

British Library Cataloguing in Publication Data

Gorringe, T. J.
God's theatre: a theology of providence.
1. God. Providence
I. Title
231.5

ISBN 0-334-02493-5

Typeset at The Spartan Press Ltd, Lymington, Hants
and printed in Great Britain by
Clays Ltd, St Ives plc

For the students and staff
of the
Tamil Nadu Theological Seminary

CONTENTS

A congregation at prayer
telling Him what he is like:
You who can do anything
you please; who steer our courses
through secondary causation, bringing
us home safe to a good
meal and a loving family
round a contented hearth; you
who can replenish the empty
belly of Asia, so anachronising
our Lent; who, producer yourself,
can appreciate the brilliance
of our performance, continue this care
since never on to the platform
of a star stepped a species
more deserving.
           Does God listen
to them, crouched as he is
over the interminable problem
of how not to cheat, when the hell-born
spirit appears to be winning?

R.S. Thomas, *The Echoes Return Slow*

PREFACE

I have dedicated this book to the Tamil Nadu Theological Seminary, a community which, in its situation and stance within India, remains my most important theological teacher. A sacramental thank you for a gift beyond price. Doing so gives me an opportunity to respond briefly to critics and friends who have told me that there is not enough of 'India' in my writing.

I am quite certain that, under the divine providence, we are called to cherish particularity – which is to say the life giving things in particular cultures, including their languages. We cherish particularity, however, (and many still confuse this 'cherishing' with 'patriotism') only insofar as it helps us cherish the whole. The Christian gospel is addressed to all people and presupposes that human problems are fundamentally the same in every culture. As an unknown writer put it near the beginning of the Christian story, for a Christian every native land is a foreign land and every foreign land a native land. 'For me the eucharist is my homeland' a Japanese Christian said to me as we met to worship in the Dom in Bonn. This fact makes me profoundly wary of 'regional' or sectional theologies. The old name for regional theologies was polytheism, a form of worship which legitimated murderous struggles between groups vying for power (and Karl Barth pointed out that the war theologies of the First World War were effectively polytheistic). Gustavo Gutiérrez tells us that the difference between Latin American liberation theology and Western theology is that they have different agendas: the former addresses poverty and oppression, and the latter the scepticism of the Enlightenment. I cannot agree. Enlightenment attitudes are in part responsible for Third World poverty, and this means that liberation theology is desperately important for the rich countries of the northern hemisphere. And Indian, African, Chinese Christian theology? Methodists used to say that their theology lay in their hymns, in which case there are indeed regional styles, but any true theology will address the question of what it is that enables me to be human and this cuts across cultural boundaries. I can only say that my experience was that friends in India struggled with the necessity and impossibility of belief in God's providence exactly as I did. I hope that they can identify with what I say.

One cultural reality which is profoundly dehumanizing is patriarchy. Conscientization takes time, and I find that using the male personal pronoun for God increasingly sets my teeth on edge – more than when it first looked quietly at me from the draft of this book. Here too one goes on learning.

Any worthwhile theology puts you on the line. Do I really believe these arguments about providence? Can one live by them? By way of response I share the prayer of another teacher who has struggled with the darkness we call providence, a prayer applicable to both the individual and the human story, and a prayer I certainly seek to live by:

> Lord of life and love
> we live in the promise that
> you know our story better than we do.
> Often we see nothing in our story but darkness
> and we long for your light.
> Hold on to us in the darkness,
> for the darkness is no darkness with you.
> Bring light to our story,
> the light of your healing providence,
> the light of the coming and creation of your kingdom,
> the light which dawns in doing your will. Amen.

1

Disposing of False Friends

Belief in providence is, to adapt a phrase of David Jenkins, both necessary and impossible, absurd, but deeply human. It is not a belief required of us formally by the creeds but, much more profoundly, by our daily prayer. Belief in providence is the very structure of the religious life: belief that God acts, that he has a purpose not simply for the whole of creation but for me, that this purpose can be discerned and that, through prayer, I can put myself in the way of it. It is also the belief that I can bring every concern to God, from the wars and famines I read about in the newspaper or see on the News to the relationship difficulties I encounter, or the problems with my work, in the conviction that this will make a difference. Christianity has never understood prayer as primarily a form of spiritual hygiene, a way of attaining self-knowledge or finding spiritual courage. Christian prayer is not a form of Transcendental Meditation. On the contrary, the keynote of Jesus' teaching on prayer, as Barth insisted again and again, is 'Ask'.

Ask, and it will be given you; seek, and you will find; knock and it will be opened to you. For every one who asks receives, and he who seeks finds, and to him who knocks it will be opened. Or what man of you, if his son asks him for bread, will give him a stone? Or if he ask for a fish will give him a serpent? If you, then, who are evil, know how to give good gifts to your children, how much more will your Father who is in heaven give good things to those who ask him! (Matt. 7.7-11)

As von Balthasar puts it, the model prayer which is given to Christians, the 'Lord's prayer', is 'a beggar's prayer from start to finish'. 'One must keep on dinning into God's ears, indeed one must become a nuisance to him, begging for the "minimum for existence" . . . Total dependence on God means that the one who knocks is sure of being heard.'[1] Such prayer rests on Jesus' uncompromising insistence that God cares even for the fall of a sparrow:

> I tell you, do not be anxious about your life, what you shall eat or what you shall drink, nor about your body . . . Look at the birds of the air: they neither sow nor reap nor gather into barns, and yet your heavenly Father feeds them. Are you not of more value than they? (Matt. 6.25-6)

The absolute necessity of Christian faith in providence is embraced in these verses even if we cannot find a technical concept of providence in scripture. It is this faith, too, which underlies the gratitude for every good thing we are given in life which is likewise part of the very foundation of Christian prayer.

Over against this all embracing trust in God, which is the fabric of Christian life, stands the tyranny of chance. It may well be that statistical laws and a sufficiently large perspective help us to discern order in seemingly chance events. This is small comfort, however, to the question why this person is struck with cancer or multiple sclerosis and not that one, why the car hit this child when a fraction of a second earlier or later or two feet to the right or left would have made the difference between life and death. The human instinct is to hold God to blame. The fairness of a world of chance cannot be preached, and one is tempted to say that what cannot be preached cannot be good theology. The Franciscan Brother Juniper of Thornton Wilder's *The Bridge of San Luis Rey* traces the history of five people killed when a bridge collapses and concludes that their death was providential, coming as it did at a climactic moment for all of them. He is burned at the stake for his pains, a reaction which expresses human outrage at what is so often supposed to be 'providence'. The God of Christian faith is not like the Hindu Siva, killing and renewing in sublime metaphysical play. He wills *life*, and cannot will the death and destruction of children, nor the wasting and disfiguring diseases which afflict so many. R.S. Thomas catches the bewildered bitterness which so easily infects faith in the face of tragedy in his poem, 'The Island':

> And God said, I will build a church here
> And cause this people to worship me,
> and afflict them with poverty and sickness
> In return for centuries of hard work
> And patience. And its walls shall be hard as
> Their hearts, and its windows let in the light
> Grudgingly, as their minds so, and the priest's words be
>   drowned
> By the wind's caterwauling. All this I will do,
>
> Said God, and watch the bitterness in their eyes
> Grow, and their lips suppurate with
> Their prayers. And their women shall bring forth
> On my altars, and I will choose the best
> Of them to be thrown back into the sea.
>
> And that was only on one island.[2]

The 'problem of evil', the problem of holding together the goodness and omnipotence of God, is better described as a problem of providence. Faith requires the most complete trust in God because it is a form of love: to have faith is to be caught up in the love of the loving Father. The problem is how to live this in the face of the constant tragedy of life.

To speak of tragedy here is to take issue with Ulrich Simon who believes that we obscure the rarity of tragedy by designating as 'tragic' events which are merely sad, heart-breaking, nauseating and fatal:

> Accidents, whether experienced or observed by us, are not tragic. Disablement, genetic malformation, crippling diseases may torment the victims and destroy their families, but they are not tragic. Nor is death a tragic conclusion to life, even when it occurs suddenly or prematurely or with disastrous consequences for the survivors. Even earthquakes and floods are not tragic, though the consequences may wipe out whole communities. Even more negative is our judgement on political and military outrages. For example, the battle of the Somme devoured hundreds of thousands of soldiers without achieving any goal, but, while we may even now enter the grief

of parents and children in remembrance of what is past, we cannot give this or any other modern battle the epithet 'tragic'. Even less appropriate would be such a description for the terror of genocide.[3]

But the common usage which speaks of all these events as 'tragic' preserves by doing so the sense of the sheer waste of the potentially good, creative and beautiful which is at the heart of tragedy. This 'sheer waste' is the sub-text of history and the context of all of our lives: every newspaper and news bulletin reminds us of it. To take the Bible in one hand is to believe in the glory God intends for human beings; to take the newspaper in the other is to see this contradicted. In this experience every believer knows providence as both necessary and impossible: this necessity and impossibility is the pulse of faith.

The difficulties this generates are reflected only too clearly in classical discussions or providence. Providence has over the years collected a great many 'false friends' with which it has been confused: fate, chance, fortune, luck, foreknowledge, predestination and determinism have all been conflated with providence at some time or other. This confusion is partly due to the fact that the concept was taken over from Stoicism or other pagan sources which meant, as one who wanted to dispense with the idea put it, that its use entailed 'many disadvantages for the clear exposition of the authentic Christian faith'.[4] The kind of disadvantages Schleiermacher had in mind can be illustrated by Karl Barth's observation that 'providence', understood as belief in history and its immanent demons, was a favourite term on the lips of Adolf Hitler.[5] If we are to save belief in providence these false friends need to be disposed of, which is the aim of this first chapter. In order to do that we need first to see what might be implied by the idea in the Jewish and Christian scriptures.

God's sovereignty: the biblical foundation of providence

The word 'providence' itself is scarcely to be found in the Bible. The Hebrew word *pequddah*, meaning a 'looking after', and usually translated 'care' in the RSV, is only used to mean 'providence' once, in Job 10.12, where it is translated as such by the New English Bible. Likewise the Greek word *pronoia* is only

used twice to mean 'providence' in Wisdom of Solomon
(14.3;17.2), and in this sense not at all in the New Testament.
Nevertheless both Old and New Testaments may be read as a
sustained testimony to God's lordship over all things which is
what the biblical notion of providence amounts to.

The English word 'providence' comes to us from the Latin
version of the story of Abraham and Isaac. When the boy Isaac
asks his father, 'Where is the ram for this burnt offering?',
Abraham replies 'Deus providebit', 'God will provide'. Since
Abraham is the model of the person of faith this reply becomes a
motto which sums up the believer's complete trust in God even in
desperate circumstances. It appropriately summarizes Jesus'
teaching about the birds of the air and the lilies of the field: 'If
God so clothes the grass of the field, which today is alive and
tomorrow is thrown into the oven, will he not much more clothe
you, you of little faith?' (Matt. 5.30). To believe in providence is
then to believe in the world as created and sustained by God, and
thus as a gracious gift which is fundamentally benign and
trustworthy. It is to believe, in the words of the harvest hymn,
that 'all good gifts around us come from heaven above' and to
take this as the basis for a life of thankfulness. 'Thou makest
springs gush forth in the valleys' wrote the psalmist:

> they flow between the hills,
> they give drink to every beast of the field;
> the wild asses quench their thirst . . .
> Thou dost cause the grass to grow for the cattle,
> and plants for man to cultivate,
> that he may bring forth food from the earth,
> and wine to gladden the heart of man.
>
> (Ps. 104. 10-11,14-15)

The psalmist speaks for all believers for whom providence is
therefore, in the first instance, God's benevolent lordship over all
creation.

But then, even more importantly, God is viewed as controlling
historical events. He 'calls' Israel out of Egypt, promises them
freedom and the land of Canaan, and uses Assyria, or Nebuchad-
nezzar or Cyrus to execute his will. Amos formulates extremely
strong affirmations of God's control of all events. YHWH asks:

Did I not bring up Israel from the land of
Egypt, and the Philistines from Caphtor and
the Syrians from Kir? (Amos 9.7)

The so-called 'Court History' of David illustrates with great
subtlety the way in which God's purpose is achieved through
events which can be given completely naturalistic explanations. If
we look at the account of the defeat of Absalom's rebellion we read
how Hushai, who is loyal to David, agrees to stay in Jerusalem both
to oppose the rebel counsellor Ahitophel and to pass on informa-
tion through the priests. Ahitophel and Hushai give competing
advice, and the story runs: 'And Absalom and all the men of Israel
said, "The counsel of Hushai the Archite is better than the counsel
of Ahithophel". For the Lord had ordained to defeat the good
counsel of Ahithophel so that the Lord might bring evil upon
Absalom' (II Sam.17.14). God's purpose is accomplished through
discussions which have nothing of the miraculous about them but
which, on the surface, are nothing but the tired scheming of an
attempted coup. It is in this way, rather than through the turning
back of the waters of the Reed Sea, that countless biblical stories
depict God as the 'lord of history'.

Finally, believers through the ages have sought divine guidance
for their own affairs. Belief in providence is belief that God is not
only the lord of history but the lord of *my* history, that God is
concerned with individuals. So the history of Israel begins when
God says to Abram, 'Go from your country and your kindred and
your father's house to the land that I will show you' (Gen.12.1).
Similarly Moses is sent to Pharaoh to liberate the people of Israel;
Saul is called and then rejected; David is anointed by Samuel;
Nathan is sent to David; Amos is called whilst going about his
ordinary business; Jeremiah is called in Anathoth. In his missionary travels Paul intended to go to Bithynia 'but the Spirit of Jesus
did not allow them . . . And a vision appeared to Paul in the night: a
man of Macedonia was standing beseeching him and saying,
"Come over to Macedonia and help us", (Acts 16.9). Throughout
the Bible God is said to have a purpose for specific individuals
which can be discerned and then acted upon.

Especially noteworthy in the scriptural accounts of God's rule is
the way in which God is seen to turn human wickedness or folly to
his own purposes. The classical illustration of this is to be found in

the story of Joseph. Joseph is sold into slavery by his brothers, which we are intended to see as a wicked and despicable act, since slavery in Egypt is the paradigm of the situation God does not will for his people. But when the brothers come begging for food and Joseph finally reveals himself to them, he does not read them a lecture but says to them: 'Do not be distressed or angry with yourselves, because you sold me here; for God sent me before you to preserve life' (Gen.45.5). God has turned human wickedness to his own purposes, the preservation of life. This story functions as a model for understanding the redemptive death of Jesus. Like Joseph's brothers Judas and Pilate and the High Priests act wickedly and yet they are, as Bengel described them, the 'executors of the New Testament'. Through their wickedness human redemption is accomplished. In the same way the cowardice or folly of Abraham, in pretending Sarah was his sister (Gen.12;20) or the deceit of Jacob (Gen.27), or the adultery of David (II Sam.12) are all turned to good. Church tradition developed this theme in the theology of the Easter exultet which praises God for the 'happy fault' which accounted for 'such and so great a Redeemer'. Providence, then, is discerned in the way in which God turns the flank of human evil, using it for his great purpose, that there may be life 'in all its fullness' (John 10.10).

The threefold rule over creation, history and the lives of individuals, directed especially to the overcoming of evil, constitutes the pattern of providence in scripture. It is clear that it lies behind the later scholastic distinction between general, special, and most special providence, where the former refers to the orderly government of the universe through the laws of nature, and the latter two speak of God's 'interventions' particularly in miracle, and particularly on behalf of the individual. The division is both obvious and helpful, though many formulations of 'general' providence need scrutiny. We cannot too often recall Calvin's splendid dictum that 'providence consists in action', and this is not compatible with the absentee landlord that some accounts of general providence make God out to be. The activity of God, said Calvin, 'is not the vain, indolent, slumbering omnipotence which sophists feign, but vigilant, efficacious, energetic and ever active – not an omnipotence which may only act as a general principle of confused motion, as in ordering a stream to keep within the channel once prescribed for it, but one which is intent on individual and special movements'.[6] From this point of view we could say that, whilst it is helpful to make distinctions between nature, history and the individual, there is only special providence and it is misleading to suppose that there is any other form.

The Church of Scotland's statement of faith accurately summarizes the biblical account of providence in affirming that 'God governs all things and overrules all events for perfectly wise and loving ends'. But how are we to understand this 'governing' and 'overruling'? Much of the problem with classical statements of providence stems from quite natural deductions drawn from the metaphor of rule or sovereignty, what Krister Stendahl has called the dangerous 'precipitate' of the metaphor.[7] The notion of God's rule is the particular concern of the fourth chapter but there are a number of related confusions we wish to dispose of at once, beginning with the ideas of predestination and fate.

Providence and predestination

Perhaps surprisingly the doctrine with which providence is most frequently elided is that of *predestination*, an elision illustrated by both Aquinas and Calvin.

For Aquinas providence is the planning of things to an end, 'a kind of plan (ratio) in the mind of the provider' and predestination is part of providence. 'The planned sending of a rational creature to the end which is eternal life is termed predestination, for to predestine is to send. And so it is clear that predestination as regards what it does objectively is a part of Providence.'[8] Predestination is 'that part of Providence which relates to those who are ordained to be saved'.[9] Calvin, on the other hand, whilst treating of providence and predestination in quite different volumes of the *Institutes* nevertheless felt constrained by the biblical texts which speak of God's sovereignty to argue that 'all events so proceed from (God's) determinate counsel that nothing happens fortuitously'.[10] Every event is governed by God's incomprehensible counsel, his 'eternal decree' according to which 'what from eternity he had foreseen, approved, decreed, he prosecutes with unvarying uniformity'.[11] In a discussion of the biblical language of 'hardening' he entirely rejects the distinction between God's will and permission introduced as early as Origen because 'the Holy Spirit distinctly says that the blindness and infatuation are inflicted by the just judgment of God'.

> The sum of the whole is this – since the will of God is said to be the cause of all things, all the counsels and actions of men must be held to be governed by his providence; so that he not only exerts his power in the elect, who are guided by the Holy Spirit, but also forces the reprobate to do him service.[12]

Both providence and predestination therefore are equally expositions of God's eternal decree – this is at the heart of both conceptions. Creation exists for human beings, human beings exist for the redemption available through the church, this redemption is the glory of God which is the purpose of creation. God's overruling of all things is for the sake of the elect chosen in his eternal decree.

It was at this point that Barth was compelled to make his fundamental break with Calvin. Whilst Calvin felt that belief in the eternal decree led to 'gratitude in prosperity, patience in adversity and incredible security for the time to come' Barth agreed with Max Weber that it actually led to a neurosis centred on God's inscrutability. But God is not inscrutable – there is nothing beyond or behind what we see in Christ. It is Christ, then, who is the elect, elected both for damnation and death in our place, and for the glory which is God's will for us, and this is the true comfort of the doctrine of election. Providence, on the other hand, does not deal with election at all but with what Aquinas called 'world government': 'By "providence" is meant the superior dealings of the Creator with his creation, the wisdom, omnipotence and goodness with which he maintains in time this distinct reality according to his will.'[13] Any elision between the two doctrines is therefore resolutely refused.

The reasons for an elision of the doctrines of providence and predestination are particularly clear in Aquinas, where a consideration of God's *knowledge* leads to the doctrine of providence as a particular instance of that knowledge, and then predestination as 'a part of providence'. God is the cause of all things through his mind (*per suum intellectum*); the idea of each and every effect must pre-exist in him; therefore the divine mind must preconceive the whole *ratio* of things and this *ratio* is providence. Considerations of providence also tend inevitably to move from 'general' to 'special' and 'most special' (i.e. individual), and the divine plan for the individual becomes again an example of predestination. If, in spite of this, we insist that providence and predestination are quite distinct this will rest, as Barth has shown, on a re-thinking of what is meant by *election*. Election is not the drawing up of detailed plans for every individual in history, so that, as Calvin imagined it, the adequacy or otherwise of the amount of milk a mother has for her baby is part of providence, nor even for specific peoples in history. Election is, in the first instance, God's option for what is other than himself, God's 'Yes' to creation. In this case it is not that predestination is a part of providence but the other way round, that providence is *pars predestinationis*, part of the doctrine of election, the working out of God's 'choice' to share his being.

Providence, fate and determinism

The habit of reading providence in terms of the operation of an omnipotent will also help explain why theologians of the stature of Augustine and Aquinas can use the concept of 'fate' and confuse it with providence. That this confusion is not a dead issue is instanced by the equivalence in contemporary speech of the expressions 'tempting fate' and 'tempting providence'. The same equation is evident in Brother Juniper's reflection, the moment after the bridge collapses in Wilder's novel, that 'Either we live by accident and die by accident, or we live by plan and die by plan'.

In an extended discussion in his *City of God* Augustine rejects the popular, astrological, understanding of fate but keeps the term, erroneously tracing the meaning of 'fatum' to the verb 'fari', to speak in Ps.61.11: 'God has spoken once'. 'Once' means immovably and signifies that God knows all that is to happen and leaves nothing unordered. He takes issue with Cicero, who felt the need to deny divine foreknowledge in order to preserve human freedom. Augustine's answer to this is to make foreknowledge analytic to the being of God: 'a being who does not know all the future is certainly not God'.[14]

In the famous discussion in Book Four of *De Consolatione* Boethius takes a still more positive attitude towards fate. Providence he defines as the divine *ratio* arranging all things, whilst fate is 'the planned order inherent in things subject to change through the medium of which Providence binds everything to its own allotted place'.

> Providence includes all things at the same time, however diverse or infinite, while Fate controls the motion of different individual things in different places and in different times. So the unfolding of the plan in time when brought together as a unified whole in the foresight of God's mind is Providence; and the same unified whole when dissolved and unfolded in the course of time is Fate (4.6).

Here 'fate' appears to refer to the causal nexus, the rules which constitute an orderly universe (more or less what Tillich in this century called 'destiny'). Its hold is less over pure intelligences, which stand 'nearest to the primary divinity' and greater the further things are removed from that divinity. It is an order which 'restrains by its own unchangeableness changeable things, which otherwise might run hither and thither at random'.

Aquinas draws on Boethius' discussion and agrees that 'fate' refers to the series of secondary causes. But 'the divine power or will can be called fate, as being the cause of fate'. 'Fate' refers to the fact that anything God foreknows will happen will certainly do so. What God foreknows must be: the ordained cause of things is immutable.[15]

The issue of whether we speak of fate or providence in the same breath is by no means trivial. Hinduism, which is no longer confined to the Indian sub-continent, still subscribes to belief in karma, an immutable ordering of all things to the smallest detail, whilst astrology enjoys a continuing popularity in the West, reputedly in the highest places.[16] What the missionary theologian A.G.Hogg said of karma applies equally to fate: if the law of karma be true, then history is robbed of its deepest meaning.[17] Both 'fate' and 'karma' mean remorseless, unalterable destiny, a conception incompatible with the Christian gospel for which, as we have seen, 'providence consists in action'. In the face of all fatalism belief in providence is the counter assertion of faith: it speaks of the living God who hears his people and answers their cry and this means that there is no place for the concept of fate in Christian discourse.

Equally, it has to be said, there is no place for any form of determinism, whether philosophical, theological or psychological. The most cogent objections to determinism have always been moral, though if D. J. Bartholomew is right that a deterministic universe would be unlikely to be complex enough to support intelligent life this would be a devastating counter argument from natural science.[18] Classical anti-determinist arguments have mostly been variations of Kant's insistence that 'ought' implies 'can', and that therefore there must be a causality of freedom, and that even if the non-animate world is determined this cannot apply to human beings. People cannot be blamed for that for which they are not responsible. William James distinguished between a soft and a hard determinism, the first of which admitted an element of moral freedom, the latter of which did not. In the context of the theological debate this is not such a helpful distinction, as Augustine, Luther and Calvin all see the need to assert human freedom even when their fundamental theological tenets do not allow it. Perhaps we could, rather, distinguish between immanent determinism, the determinations we know through psychology and sociology, and transcendent determinism, determination through an omnipotent being. As far as the former goes, whilst there is a great deal of evidence for the extent to which we *are* determined in our actions and choices none of this amounts to a thesis of rigorous determinism, and all legal systems continue to presuppose responsibility. A thoroughgoing determinism on this level would make all moral distinctions irrational. The very existence of an ordered society is to some extent a disproof of the idea. By the same token a god who determined all things could not ground moral distinctions, Augustine and his followers notwithstanding. What makes God the world Ruler, said Barth, as opposed to all false gods and idols is 'the very fact that his rule is determined and limited: self-determined and self-limited, but determined and limited none the less'.[19] Knowledge of this self-limitation derives from the cross, for if everything were rigorously determined what could the cross be but a piece of spectacular, though indecent, theatre? On the contrary the 'necessity' of the cross, frequently spoken about by New Testament authors, is God's refusal to overrule human history. If the cross is our guide, God is no determinist.

Providence and chance

The polar opposite to the absolute determinism of fate is the notion that there is no discernible purpose in events but that, as Ecclesiastes puts it, 'the race is not to the swift, nor the battle to the strong, nor bread to the wise, nor riches to the intelligent, nor favour to men of skill; but time and chance happen to them all' (Eccles. 9.11). For Calvin it was this which was the real challenge to faith[20] and he would agree with the French biologist Jacques Monod that to ascribe the course of evolution entirely to chance would mean the denial of theism. Significantly Monod allowed that the theist's only possible response was the one which Calvin actually adopted, namely that God determined every single event.[21] Some contemporary theologians, however, have seen in chance not a threat but a promise. An early essay exploring this position is the physicist theologian W.G.Pollard's *Chance and Providence*, published in 1958. Starting from the 'Uncertainty Principle' of quantum physics Pollard suggested that it was at the sub atomic level, where events are not determined, that God's providence was exercised, though he stressed that the 'how' of this action was inconceivable. Invoking the analogy of the Bohr complementarity principle, according to which light can be understood now in terms of waves and now in terms of particles he suggested that providence and chance might be reconciled in the same kind of way – the two are just different perspectives on the same set of events. The effect of this proposal is, of course, to rule out real chance, for what Pollard means by chance is simply the openness of events at the sub atomic level for God's direction. For Pollard 'the recognition of providence in the chances and accidents of the tumultuous unfolding of events converts what otherwise can only seem the dark fruits of an inscrutable fate into the smiling face of destiny'.[22] It could be Calvin speaking.

More recently the statistician D.J.Bartholomew has provided a much more sophisticated study of the theological implications of a universe where chance is a fundamental factor.[23] Departing from his definitions a little we can distinguish between three senses of chance. There is Aristotle's definition of chance as the intersection of two unconnected causal chains (for example the decision of a child to visit a friend and a motorist taking a drink too many) which we can call *real chance* (Bartholomew calls this 'accident'). There is then what we call in conversation '*pure chance*', one damn thing after another, complete purposelessness, which is what Monod thought he found in evolution. Finally, there is what Bartholomew calls *pseudo chance* where what appears to be a chance event, like the outcome of Australia winning the toss, could actually be calculated by knowledge of initial determining conditions such as the angle of the coin, velocity, force etc. Bartholomew points out that scientific work since Monod does not favour the thesis that the world we have is the product of pure chance. Chaos is not transformed into order by good luck or pure chance but statistical sciences reveal a nisus towards order in what is apparently random. Statistical science is only possible at all because in all sorts of fields, from genetics to consumer spending, a sufficiently large collection of purely 'random' facts or data reveal under analysis simplicity, stability and order. Real chance, in Aristotle's sense, turns out to be the seed bed of order. Were we to set out deliberately to create chaos, Bartholomew argues, the law of large numbers would still apply and regularities on a large scale would soon appear. Thus the idea of 'pure chance' is an illusion caused by inability to see the wood for the trees. Further, chance often has a positive use in human affairs, for example to ensure a non partial result as in tossing to see who starts a game or 'drawing the short straw' (cf Acts 1.26). By analogy, might not God have, as it were, designed a universe in which chance plays a large role? Many advantages attach to a universe where chance is a fundamental factor. The unexpected stimulates our creative potential and 'provides both the stimulus and the testing to promote our spiritual evolution'.[24] The creation must have a built in capacity to recover from what human beings might do to it, and random processes have this capacity. Survival depends on variety and adaptability and the random element in the reproductive system guarantees this. The universe must witness to the 'fairness' or justice of God and a world where it rains on both just and unjust does this. Again, only a universe which includes chance, Bartholomew argues, could be a ground for free and intelligent life. Chance allows for human freedom and for God to respond to the misuse of that freedom without overruling affairs. Following Arthur Peacocke he suggests that chance mechanisms such as the rapid and frequent randomization possible at the molecular level of the DNA, would be an efficient means for God to 'explore the creative potential' of the universe. This picture allows us to say that God chose to create random processes knowing that order would be the result, but without planning every event in advance.

All these are extremely helpful suggestions for without question chance is a fact of our experience of life, and yet needs to be coordinated with purpose to avoid Monod's conclusions. Providence is incompatible with pure chance but not with real chance. Real chance, however, is not yet providence but, perhaps, the framework within which God has chosen to operate. The need to spell out what we mean by providence remains. But perhaps we do not need the concept at all. A number of contemporary theologians have followed a hint in Lutheran Orthodoxy and prefer to talk of *continuous creation*.

Creation and providence

There are two forms which an elision of creation and providence may take. The first is Deist, and we have a re-statement of this position in Maurice Wiles' Bampton Lectures, *God's Action in the World*. As he acknowledges in his final paragraph the 'action' of the title is a little over generous as a description of what God does. It is in fact restricted to the setting up of those initial conditions of creation which make possible the emergence of a 'genuinely free human recognition and response to what is God's intention in the creation of the world'.[25] The reason we do not simply eliminate the idea of God's action is because our lives, and above all saintly lives, are part of God's act and purpose in bringing the world into existence. Wiles speaks of this as a 'continuing creation' but such a description seems to be illegitimate as none of the 'subacts' which follow the master act of creation can properly be ascribed to God. These 'subacts' consist of the regular patterns of the physical world, breaches of these normal patterns, sometimes called 'miracles', and human actions either within or without the community of faith. In none of these cases does Wiles believe that we are free to speak of divine intervention. To do so either implies an improper understanding of created reality, or it involves us in insoluble problems in face of the problem of evil, or it 'opens the floodgates to fanaticism'.

Eighteenth-century Deism is generally felt to be the product of an overweening human self-confidence, a rationalism which does not take sin seriously. Maurice Wiles' version, on the other hand, arises from what we can call the 'moral case against providence'. The God in whom we believe does not tyrannize over creation but allows it autonomy. The religious life is thus a matter of discerning God's purposes in creation and seeking to act accordingly. This position cuts the Gordian knot of the necessity and impossibility of belief in providence. It makes both the problem of evil, and the problems of reconciling grace and free will, far less intractable. What stands against it is what has always been recognized to be its religious inadequacy and its failure to do justice to the foundation of Christian tradition, scripture. Wiles twice quotes a remark of Walter Kasper's to the effect that a God who no longer plays an active role in the world is a dead God. In reply he speaks of the worshipper's 'grateful awareness of God's all pervasive and sustaining presence' – but this is a presence which does nothing. It is reminiscent of Whitehead's 'Fellow Sufferer who understands', which is in no way adequate as a characterization of YHWH, the God who raises Jesus of Nazareth from the dead. To refer to the resurrection here underlines the fact that complex positions on revelation and scripture underlie Wiles' whole argument. If these are rejected then perhaps we need to go back to necessity and impossibility, the living tension of Christian belief, the Gordian knot which has been cut too quickly and too easily. To do that, and to seek an answer to the moral case against providence, is the purpose of the present discussion.

The second kind of elision between creation and providence is quite different, preferring to think of God's continuous *action*. Its origins can be found as early as the thirteenth century, with Aquinas. For him 'creation' means the causing or producing of things whereas 'providence' is 'the exemplar of things ordained to their purpose', God's foreknowledge of the whole pattern of things moving to their end. This looks distinct enough until we learn that God causes things through his mind and will *like an artist* (an extremely important analogy).[26] But in that case when we speak of creation we are speaking of 'the exemplar forms existing in the divine mind' just as we are in the case of providence. Another important analogy, between the *design* of a government and its *execution*, likewise confuses the two for the preservation of the world in providence is 'a continuation of that action by which (God) gives existence' – in other words, of creation.[27]

From a very different perspective Schleiermacher also elided the notions of creation and preservation since both of them were equally expressions of the sense of absolute dependence. He saw 'no sufficient reason for retaining this division instead of the original expression (i.e. of dependence) which is so natural'.[28] Likewise Paul Tillich prefers to speak of God's 'directing creativity' rather than of creation and providence separately. 'Providence is not interference; it is creation. It uses all factors, both those given by freedom and those given by destiny, in creatively directing everything towards its fulfilment.'[29]

Given this degree of proximity in the tradition it is no surprise therefore that, in the face of our knowledge of evolution, many contemporary theologians opt to talk of 'continuous creation' rather than of providence. Because the universe is unfinished, argues Ian Barbour, we must recognize that creation refers not to one moment but to every moment in time, and this, he believes, is congenial to the biblical doctrine for which the idea of creation out of nothing is only a very late arrival.[30] Creation and providence were traditionally distinguished, he argues, first, on the grounds of a *temporal* distinction between God's initial act and his subsequent acts, secondly, through an *ontological* distinction between God's *actus purus* and his action through secondary causes, and finally, through a distinction between God's absolute sovereignty on the one hand and the way this is qualified by human freedom and the regularity of nature on the other. These distinctions, Barbour suggests, appeal to an immobilist conception of the world which read the Genesis account literally. The idea of continuous creation, by contrast, corresponds to contemporary scientific views, can be developed from a text like Psalm 104, and is equally an expression of God's sovereignty and freedom.

Does it matter? Is there anything at stake in the traditional distinction between creation and providence? There is: it is a question of the freedom of grace and the freedom (contingence) of creation. We have to distinguish between creation as an initial act, an act of origination, on the one hand, and *creativity as a quality of all God's actions on the other*. The language of continuous creation can be a way of saying that God always interacts with his creation and does so in a creative way. This does not fulfil the same function as the assertion of an original act of creation, which is to answer what Heidegger called the fundamental metaphysical question, '*Why is there anything rather than nothing?*'. The doctrine of creation from nothing is concerned on the one hand to root all things in grace, in God's free and non-necessary decision to share his love. On the other hand, as Torrance has emphasized, it guarantees the contingence of the created world. If there were a necessary and timeless relation between God and the world, as some versions of continuous creation imply, then it would be 'virtually impossible to distinguish nature from God', so that both divine and created freedom would be denied.[31] At the same time it is really not the case that the idea of creation 'in the beginning' presupposes an 'immobilist' framework of thought. It is much rather a question of recognizing that here theological and scientific languages are doing very different things. When the Priestly writer talks about God 'finishing' his work of creation, he is not doing wrong or primitive science but making a faith statement about the perfection of creation for its purpose. The nineteenth-century controversies over evolution arose from a failure to differentiate these languages. It is also not the case, as Barbour maintains, that the existential significance of the doctrines of creation and providence is the same. On the contrary one speaks of the mystery of our origin and the other speaks of the mystery of the strange and unbalanced mixture of pain and beauty which constitutes our iife. It is the latter with which we are concerned in providence. But Barbour voices another widespread contemporary concern in feeling that the recognition that theology and science speak separate languages can be pushed to the extreme of a total separation between them so that we are left with a dualistic portrayal of reality.[32] Granted that danger, we have to ask about the contribution the physical sciences might make to the doctrine of providence. To this question we now turn.

2

Can We Do Theology by Doing Science?

Once upon a time there was a philosopher called Descartes, and a scientist called Newton. Together they represented a world view according to which nature was a closed mechanistic system of cause and effect, in which God could at best be understood as the first mover of the cosmic process. From their thought stemmed a 'deistic disjunction' between God and the world which made the task of theology more or less impossible. Then along came Einstein with the realization that $E = mc^2$ and this made it possible once again to do theology as it ought to be done.

I caricature only a little. We have been repeatedly told in the past thirty years that science, and especially the new physics, has profound implications for theology. Scorning Moltmann's attempt to write on creation with 'only an occasional and cursory reference to scientific insight' Polkinghorne writes that 'It is as idle to suppose that one can satisfactorily speak about the doctrine of creation without taking into account the actual nature of the world, as it would be to think that the significance of the world could be exhaustively conveyed in the scientific description of its physical processes.'[1] The wilful ignorance of the theologians means, according to Polkinghorne, that theology cannot simply be left to them. Faced with rather similar claims as he set about the Prolegomena to his *Church Dogmatics* Karl Barth denied that theology was in any way dependent on the natural

sciences. 'As regards method it has nothing to learn in their
school', he wrote.[2] When he came to tackle the doctrine of
creation he decided to eschew the 'dilettante entanglements'
which an engagement with scientific questions would have
brought. At first he had felt that dealing with the scientific
problems would have been necessary,

> but I later saw that there can be no scientific problems,
> objections or aids in relation to what Holy Scripture and the
> Christian Church understand by the divine work of
> creation . . . There is free scope for natural science beyond
> what theology describes as the work of the Creator. And
> theology can and must move freely where science which is
> really science, and not secretly a pagan *Gnosis* or religion, has
> its appointed limit.[3]

He concluded with the view that 'future workers in the field of
Christian doctrine of creation will find many problems worth
pondering in defining the point and manner of this twofold
boundary'. This boundary has been the special concern of
T. F. Torrance in the past twenty years, of Pannenberg from a
rather different point of view, and more recently of the physicist
theologian John Polkinghorne. Their arguments can be summar-
ized in three points relating to method, the revival of natural
theology and the importance of understanding God's engagement with the world.[4]

Theology and scientific method

There are in the first place a batch of claims about the relatedness
of theological and scientific *method*. Torrance has taken from
Barth the point that theology has its own proper object which
dictates its own proper mode of enquiry. To allow the object to
determine the enquiry is, in his view, truly scientific procedure.
On the other hand dialogue with the natural sciences ensures that
theology does not remain hide bound by outdated world views. A
slightly different claim is made by Polkinghorne who wishes to
emphasize that insofar as theology relies on the element of
judgment and 'evaluation by the knower' it is not *toto caelo*
different from science. Science 'is not different in kind from other
kinds of human understanding but only different in degree'.[5]

Both theology and science involve corrigible attempts to understand experience and both are concerned with exploring and submitting to the way things are.

The concern of Wolfhart Pannenberg, in his *Theology and the Philosophy of Science*, is to defend the scientific respectability of theology as a university discipline.[6] He goes back to Barth's old opponent, Heinrich Scholz, who had proposed that there were a number of criteria which had to be satisfied for any discipline to count as a science, especially that there be statements whose truth is asserted, that its propositions relate to a single field of study and cohere, and that these statements can be tested. Like Scholz Pannenberg feels that Barth's appeal to God's revealed Word as the proper object of theology is illegitimate because Barth has no means of showing (beyond repeated assertion) that the 'God' of whom he speaks is not simply a postulate of our consciousness. Barth's theological method is 'the furthest extreme of subjectivism made into a theological position'.[7] A science of *faith*, as Barth understood theology, is not yet *science* but a form of positivism. Pannenberg proposes to remedy this by understanding theology as the study of Christianity in so far as it is the science of God, and understanding 'God' as 'the reality which determines all things'. If that is the case then it is 'all objects' which offer us possible traces of God. 'Theology as the science of God would then mean the study of the totality of the real from the point of view of the reality which ultimately determines it both as a whole and in its parts.'[8] But since not even a Hegelian theologian can achieve this and 'models of totality of meaning' are only available to us in particular experiences then we come down to Christianity and the claim that the Christian gospel provides us with a more illuminating way of making sense of all of our experience than other religions. The historical religions are 'anticipatory experiences of the totality of meaning of reality'. Theology can count as a genuine science, in Scholz' sense, because there is a single area of study ('postulate of coherence'), namely the historical religions, which can be tested ('postulate of control') in terms of its illuminating power and in this way make truth claims ('postulate of propositions'). Theological statements are 'offered as hypotheses about the total meaning of experience, but *firstly* from the point of view of the reality which ultimately determines everything given in its still incomplete totality, and *secondly* with reference to the way in which this divine reality has made itself known in religious consciousness'.[9] The mouse of this mountain of labours is that the concept of God is substantiated by the insights it provides into our own lives. If it is this which frees us from positivism then so be it but almost any theology can be validated in these terms.

The possibility of natural theology

The second theme common to most writers concerned with the boundary of science and theology is an attempt to re-state natural theology. Torrance argues that natural theology, which here means theological reflection on the natural world, constitutes the 'epistemological framework' of theology in much the same way that geometry functions as the epistemological structure in the heart of physics.[10] By this he appears to mean that we need to understand the world with which God interacts in order to understand his action. Polkinghorne endorses this and, in a way congenial to Aquinas, argues that pattern and process lie at the heart of any attempt to construct a natural theology.[11]

The arguments which reappear are the old friends soundly beaten by Kant but not quite dead, the arguments from design and contingency. Thus we can argue that the universe the new physics discloses to us points us to God in a way that the older physics did not. According to Torrance the combination of unpredictability and lawfulness which contemporary physics discloses to us 'is the signature of the Creator in the depths of contingent being'.[12] For Polkinghorne the world science describes to us is one of order, intelligibility, potentiality and tightly-knit character 'consonant with the idea that it is the expression of the will of a Creator, subtle, patient and content to achieve his purposes by the slow unfolding of process inherent in those laws of nature which, in their regularity, are but pale reflections of his abiding faithfulness'.[13] Behind this kind of argument are a set of assumptions about the way in which creation 'must' bear the marks of the Creator, 'however veiled' they may be, so that we can clarify our understanding of God by looking at the world he creates.[14] Likewise we have the (unobjectionable) axiom that 'all truth is God's truth' and the perfectly reasonable conviction that we need to be freed from out-moded thought forms in order to comprehend the deeper truths of revelation. In terms of method this means that we can begin from science and see later how the picture science gives us can be squared with revelation. An appeal to axioms such as these is not necessarily illegitimate since, if the frequently invoked formulation of Gödel's theorem is to be believed, such axioms stand at the beginning of all forms of human enquiry.

The same axiom about creation reflecting the Creator grounds the claim that the rationality of the universe disclosed to us by science leads us to praise God. As a matter of fact the argument from design always seems to have functioned in this way, as both Psalm 19 and many hymns, especially those of the eighteenth century, show.

Somewhat different is the re-statement of the cosmological argument in terms of the demands of the rationality of the contingent universe. The open or indeterminate nature of scientific propositions which cannot be completely formalized within closed systems means that 'their contingent intelligibility by its very nature requires to be completed beyond itself'.[15] Polkinghorne speaks of the way in which science 'almost irresistibly' points beyond itself. Torrance often appeals to Polanyi for a view of reality in which progressively higher levels call for different and non reducible explanations. Thus chemistry presumes physics, but cannot be accounted for in terms of it; biology presupposes chemistry; human sciences presuppose all these levels. The appeal to God is the appeal to a level which makes sense of all these. Conversely Polkinghorne claims that 'all non-scientific levels of meaning are ultimately subverted by a thorough-going scientific reductionism'.[16]

One of the standard objections to natural theology was that it led us to the God of the philosophers, rather than to the God of Abraham, Isaac and Jacob. Paul Fiddes argues that this objection no longer obtains because evolutionary theory discloses a world which must be conceived as a 'community of relationships', 'a macro-process that requires as much sacrifice and pain as the building of any human community'.[17] For the first time in Christian history reflection on God derived from creation leads us to a 'theology of the cross'. Behind this argument lies a certain sympathy with the pan-mentalism of the process theologians, and it is by no means clear that this view does not involve some version of the 'pathetic fallacy', resting on a misuse of analogies drawn from the human world used to image the non-human world. This will be discussed further in the next chapter.

Arguing for a revived natural theology, as a statistician D.J.Bartholomew nevertheless warns against simplistic moves from science to God. Thus he rejects what he calls the 'significance test', which argues that the probability of the world turning out as it does is so small that we are forced to postulate a guiding intelligence. Arguments from probability, however, cannot demonstrate the probability of God existing but show rather *how prior beliefs should be changed by evidence*. 'If a person insists on assigning a zero prior probability to some hypothesis, then no amount of empirical evidence can move him. If, however, he is prepared to allow some probability, no matter how small, then given sufficient evidence, his view can be changed.'[18] All that we are entitled to claim is that, as the cosmologist Paul Davies puts it, it is difficult to escape the conclusion that 'something is going on'. We are left with a rather weak variant of the argument from design: 'For intelligent beings to have appeared capable of reasoning about their origins and destiny it apparently required such a delicate adjustment of the initial conditions, that it is scarcely credible that this happy conjunction could have arisen without some prior intention.'[19]

The engagement of God with space and time

The third of the three themes shared by Torrance and Polkinghorne is the proper insistence that it is in and through space and time that God makes himself known. Theology has to be concerned with what the sciences say because God's self-revelation 'carries with it spatio-temporal coefficients' as Torrance puts it: 'The truth into which we inquire is intimated to us by some aspect of objective reality.'[20] Polkinghorne makes the same point in saying that the world is not to be divided into the sacred and profane. There is *one* world and both theology and science seek understanding of its reality.

But does it follow from the fact that God engages with the world that we learn about God in learning about the world? The problem is that, as Herbert McCabe insists, God is not a member of this or any other universe.[21] Torrance make the same point in saying that we cannot coordinate the divine and the human in one language and that therefore there is not only a false but also a proper and essential dualism.[22] In order to consider this problem we need to look at two of the classical foci for God's engagement, the incarnation and the resurrection.

To say that Jesus was fully human is to say that his body, like all other forms of matter, is composed of quarks and gluons, or however the building blocks of matter are described. To say 'The Word became flesh' is to say that God took matter upon himself. What happened to this body at the resurrection? In David Jenkins's famous phrase, the resurrection is not a 'conjuring trick with bones' – it is not God re-shuffling the atomic pack. The resurrection of Jesus is a break with the law of the conservation of energy. When we die our bodies either rot or are burned and their atomic structure feeds back into the energy quota of the universe. We are not saying that God 'did' something with the corpse of Jesus, perhaps with a dose of high level radiation. In thinking about the resurrection we are doing theology, not physics. What happens at the resurrection is described by the New Testament writers as a 'new creation'. The body of Jesus is assumed into the divine life, 'divinized' as Athanasius says. The 'new creation' asserts both continuity and discontinuity. There is continuity: the risen body bears the marks of the cross. It is the story of Jesus, his identity, which is taken up into God. In this way the old creation is affirmed. But there is discontinuity: this creation is really *new*. The resurrection body does not behave like an earthly body. It does not have an atomic structure but, as Paul puts it, is 'clothed in immortality'. The *possibility* that this might be the case, that this is not a fairy story or, as theologians concerned to be scientific sometimes call it, a 'myth', rests on the absolute otherness of God. It is something that can be argued for purely and simply on theological grounds, on the grounds, as Barth said, of God's self-revelation. Physics has nothing whatsoever to contribute here. None of the instruction Polkinghorne feels would be of assistance to the theologian would, in point of fact, be of any avail. Torrance wishes to say that the resurrection is the *redemption* of space and time, and that in it they are not abrogated or transcended but healed and restored.[23] Perhaps the new creation *is* the healing and restoring of the old but, if the resurrection stories are anything to go by, this involves their being transcended and their limitations at least being abrogated. The new creation is not simply *another* creation but the situation where God is 'all in all', where we see 'face to face'. The distance from God signified by the expulsion from paradise no longer obtains.

But how is it with the incarnation? Here, after all, God takes a body, the basic constituents of matter, upon himself. The man Jesus could have been bruised, cut, operated upon, psychoanalysed, and at the end of the day was in fact murdered. Does physics help us to understand how this can be the case? It seems to me, again, that it does not. We learn from the incarnation that God *affirms* the created order. We learn that it is *possible* for him to interact with it at the deepest level. Doubtless the reason for that is that the universe is God's free creation, as opposed to being a resistant mass of alien material, which is the form of dualism theology has ultimately to resist. Because this universe is God's free creation we can view it as profoundly *internal* to God, to appeal to the Kabbalic zimzum metaphor Moltmann has taken up.[24] We do not, however, in any way learn about what makes this interaction possible: this possibility lies in God's freedom, in his being. We have to conceive it *theologically*. Pollard's suggestion that we might conceive of God's interaction with the universe in terms of psycho-kinesis bearing on the indeterminacy of fundamental particles is exactly the kind of attempt to do theology by doing science which David Jenkins has warned us off in relation to the resurrection. It is fair enough to invoke the principle of different levels of understanding but theology does not go beyond the human sciences in the same way that these go beyond biology, or biology beyond chemistry and physics: there is an absolute qualitative distinction. There is no natural progression from creation into God. For this universe to be caught up into God involves a transition to his sphere, his space and time, 'beyond' this universe or any universe.

Mutatis mutandis the same remarks apply to creation and providence. The physical sciences are not, in fact, any help in the attempt to describe *how* God engages with his world. If we insist on this attempt we end up with a being who is not properly God, an extremely powerful cosmic engineer who might be a contemporary version of Plato's Demiurge, or Arius' Logos, but not the God of grace. As Torrance correctly points out, the physical sciences can feed our praise by revealing to us the wonder and complexity of the world in which we live. In doing this they fulfil the same function as poetry, or the experience of falling in love. If we accept the axiom that any creation will reflect its creator they may feed the argument from design, though this axiom needs scrutiny. It is not at all clear what we learn about the man Mozart from his music, or of Shakespeare from his plays, or of Rembrandt from his paintings, including the self-portraits. As Rilke said of Cezanne, he painted not 'this is how I feel', but 'this is how it is', and the greater the artist the more deeply do they seem to be concealed behind their work. 'The best dramatists explain themselves least' as Peter Brook puts it, and God seems to have created without a mass of stage directions and explanations. Polkinghorne candidly admits that a close acquaintance with cosmology need not lead a person to God: it leads the American cosmologist Steven Weinberg only to a sense of tragedy for instance.[25] The axiom also fails to reflect the distance God may have given his creation precisely as a measure of its freedom. It arises, however, from the sense of wonder which, since the days of the psalmist and the hymn writers of ancient Egypt, we know the universe has evoked in its human beholders. It is not only science but ordinary everyday human experience which points beyond itself. It is sophisticated reflection such as we find in the disillusioned Preacher of Jerusalem (Ecclesiastes) or in Hume or Jacques Monod or Weinberg which can look at the universe and see nothing but chance and therefore despair. Torrance makes the point that some world views are more congenial to Christian faith than others: doubtless this is the case, though Christian faith is not dependent on world views and we must never forget Dean Inge's warning that the person who marries the *Zeitgeist* very quickly becomes a widower. The insistence of contemporary physics on contingency is congenial to Christian theology and underwrites what theologians wish to say on the basis of revelation. More importantly a statistician like Bartholomew can show that the chance which marks reality so deeply is not 'pure chance' but the seed bed of order and that therefore discourse about divine purpose remains possible. The revolution in physics in the present century, however, might teach us caution about feeling that the last word in understanding the mysteries of the universe has been spoken. As Barth always insisted, theology has its own proper object, which is revelation and it is to that extent

independent of whatever the present state of scientific research
might happen to be. Torrance himself makes the point that
theologians were led to a new understanding of space and time
simply by following up the logic of the incarnation: we are not
dependent on physics for this, and we can just be glad that the
natural sciences at the moment seem to want to say what
theology, on other grounds, also wants to say. Again, if we feel
defensive as theologians we can be comforted by the assurance
that the methods of our study are not so fundamentally different
from those of the natural sciences though Pannenberg's attempt
to put theology on all fours with every other scientific discipline
actually fails with his very first postulate. God is not a hypothesis
to be tested, nor the 'problem' theology investigates. As Barth
replied to Scholz, 'Concept of knowledge notwithstanding, this
object of knowledge will never stand this treatment'. 'Not an iota
can be surrendered here without betraying theology.'[26]

Polkinghorne reformulates Einstein's famous mutuality of
concept and intuition thus: 'Religion without science is confined; it fails to be completely open to reality. Science without
religion is incomplete; it fails to attain the deepest possible
understanding.'[27] Of course theology cannot be obscurantist.
The theologian comes to his or her proper object, revelation, with
a mind informed by Einstein, Bohr, Prigogine, as well as by Marx,
Wittgenstein, John Berger and Iris Murdoch. The culture of the
day, including the scientific culture, is what gives us the 'spectac-
les behind the eyes' with which we understand revelation. We
have to speak about God, and try and fathom how we can speak
of God's engagement with our world, in terms of the conceptual
apparatus our culture gives us. It is our culture which provides us
with *analogies* for this talk of God, perhaps analogies which are
tremendously illuminating, and which may illuminate many
generations, as the substance and accident analogy illuminated a
great many generations as a way of conceiving God's presence in
the eucharist. Conversely a prevailing mind set can, and indeed
did, provide analogies which essentially cloud and confuse the
issue, as the 'receptacle' notion of space did for the incarnation,
according to Torrance. But analogies, be they helpful or unhelp-
ful, eventually fail, lose their conviction; they are tools which can
become outdated and pass into museums, not works of art which
can claim to be permanently illuminating. As theologians we need

to be sensitive to what science has to tell us as a way of speaking of God, but this is not to say that to write about creation a theologian must play the dilettante scientist, nor the scientist the dilettante theologian. Theological science is concerned with reality from a quite different perspective from natural science: from the perspective of the whole of reality, certainly, like the metaphysician, but more particularly from the light that God's revelation throws on reality.

Torrance wishes to argue that the new physics gets rid of the old dualisms between material existence and absolute space and time and that this makes it impossible to operate any longer with the separation between natural and revealed theology.[28] This is surely misconceived. If we argue for a 'natural theology', which we here understand as a theology derived from reflection on the created universe, it is on the grounds of a belief in God's work as Creator, in his faithfulness, and a refusal to believe that the whole universe is somehow fallen, a belief and a refusal derived primarily from revelation in Christ. The new physics naturally helps us reflect on the created universe but it does not, in itself, make a natural theology either possible or impossible. What are needed are properly *theological* categories for talking about God's interaction with created reality. A tradition which goes back at least as far as Aquinas seeks to develop these in terms of language about causality.

Divine causality

The basic categories of Aquinas' discussion of providence, for obvious reasons, are those of *knowledge, will* and *cause*. These categories follow naturally from an attempt to grasp what creation from nothing would mean. God is not the universe, and yet he posits the universe, brings it into being. If we ask 'How?' the answer appears to be, simply by willing it. Creation and providence belong intimately together because *God's being is his actual understanding.* For God, *to be* and *to know* are the same thing so God exists *as an act of knowledge* and this knowledge, when taken together with the divine will, is the cause of all things.[29] The will puts into effect what is conceived in the mind, and this 'what is conceived in the mind' is providence in the strict sense.[30]

In using the language of causality Aquinas took over Aristotle's account of material, formal, efficient and final 'causes'. The word 'cause' here is of course not used univocally. Rather, Aristotle's 'aitia' represent different types of questions which can be put to objects or events. You can ask what an object is made of, or what were the material factors involved in an event, and the answer you get denotes the 'material cause'. You can ask about the plan or design behind an object or event – which gives you the formal cause. You can ask who or what made a thing – which tells you the efficient cause. Finally, you can ask about the ultimate purpose or inner rationale of something – which describes the final cause. Significantly Aristotle did not apply this line of questioning to all type of events: he did not ask about the 'final cause' of the weather for instance. This was quite different for Aquinas for whom Aristotle's Unmoved Mover became a personal God. A mixed bag of axioms lie behind his account of God as 'cause' of all things. He presumes, for example, that things by nature reach after determinate forms (first axiom) so that an exemplar is required that it may achieve this form (second axiom); that all activity is for some good (third axiom) and that nothing can be good unless it shares some likeness with the Supreme Good, God (fourth axiom); finally that secondary causes have no independent power and always act 'in the power of the first' so that 'all things act in the power of God himself'.[31]

There are three objections to this use of the category of cause, roughly philosophical, moral, and theological. Bertrand Russell expresses the general empiricist approach to the idea of causality in describing it as 'a relic of a bygone age, surviving, like the monarchy, only because it is erroneously supposed to do no harm'.[32] Since Hume many philosophers have attempted to understand the idea of cause solely in terms of observed regularity, but this attempt has not been conspicuously successful. The *reductio ad absurdum* of Russell's attempt to eliminate the idea of cause (e1 causes e2) was his cheerful acceptance of the inference that we could say that night causes day. Of course what Aristotle ultimately presupposes in his account is that the world is intelligible and that its intelligibility can be formulated, a presupposition which is at the root of both science and common sense. Hume himself knew this. 'Principles which are permanent, irresistible and universal', he wrote, 'such as the customary transition from causes to effects . . . are the foundation of all our thoughts and actions, so that upon their removal human nature must immediately perish and go to ruin.'[33] We can then perhaps define 'cause' as follows: A cause is that intelligibility which is grasped between two events (e1 and e2) such that the intelligibility of the latter event can only be grasped in relation to the intelligibility of the former. In this sense to speak of God as the cause of all things is to say that all things ultimately find their intelligibility in God, which is part at least of the function of Aquinas' doctrine of the 'final cause'.

The second objection is bound up with the idea of God's governance through secondary causes. Aquinas maintains that whilst God is not bound to use secondary causes he generally does so in order to preserve deliberation and free choice.[34] 'The effect of divine Providence', he writes, 'is for a thing to come about not just anyhow but in its own proper style, necessarily or contingently as the case may be. What the plan of Providence has arranged to result necessarily and without fail will come about so, what too it has arranged to result contingently will come about so.' This is to give with one hand and take away with the other for whether events happen necessarily or contingently they do so 'from the unchangeable and certain order of divine providence'.[35] We must remember, says Aquinas' modern editor (Thomas Gilby), that the supreme and complete cause is not necessarily the *sole* cause, and 'the key to the situation' is found in the notion of a secondary principal cause which is free. But because God's knowledge is ultimately the cause of all things, and he is omniscient, God's omnicausality, the fact that he 'innermostly acts in all things' follows. God both foreknows and causes contingent events.[36] Gilby comments: 'A contingent thing does not arrive necessarily, yet it is necessary for it to arrive given divine foreknowledge and choice.'[37] It is difficult to resist Hume's irony at this point. It is not possible, he remarks,

> to explain distinctly, how the Deity can be the mediate cause of all the actions of men, without being the author of sin and moral turpitude. These are mysteries which mere natural and unassisted reason is very unfit to handle . . . To reconcile the indifference and contingency of human actions with prescience, or to defend absolute decrees, and yet free the Deity from

being the author of sin, has been found hitherto to exceed all the power of philosophy.[38]

Barth, who in many ways is far more Hume's successor than Hegel's, mounted a theological challenge to the concept of cause on the grounds that 'it missed completely the relation between creation and the covenant of grace'.[39] The point is well taken and it underlines that the 'intelligibility' we assert in speaking of God as cause is the intelligibility of love. This is the clue to a proper account of divine causality. Love, or grace, is the formal or final cause of creation because it is grace, the attractiveness of God, which in-forms creation and draws it to God. What we call 'Grace' is, from one point of view, the intelligibility of God. The world is, and is intelligible, because God is gracious and because grace is supreme intelligibility. It has form because form is grace-ful and it has purpose because creation is grace and grace is not meaningless but the revelation of meaning. A properly theolog-ical account of causality will be a causality of love.

For this very reason we cannot confuse natural science and theology. Herbert McCabe talks of Jesus being 'loved into being' in the womb of Mary.[40] In the same way the material universe is 'loved into being' by God. Rather than fixing on knowledge and will as the root of the divine causality we must think of love or grace. Reformulating Aquinas slightly we must say that it is God's will of love which is creative of the material world, and which continues to sustain it. That love is creative is perhaps the most fundamental form of human knowledge. The difference between the divine and human creativity of love is not only that the latter is partial and flawed, where the former is not, but that God's love brings reality, matter, the universe, into being which human love cannot do. For God it is not true that 'nothing can come out of nothing'. Humans always need a 'material cause': God does not. Again, although we shall argue later for a 'special relationship' between God and persons we have to remember that *all* being, at every level, is held in existence by God's will. To use McCabe's metaphor, the universe is sustained in being as the singer sustains her song. Because this sustaining is total it makes no sense, either, to talk of divine 'intervention' as if there were a world without God into which God sometimes stepped. Such an interventionist picture has usually been headed off by the language of immanence, language which, like many notions of providence, stems ultimately from Stoicism. Such language is too impersonal and easily suggests the Stoic idea of God as a kind of 'stuff'. Rather, we need to think of God's personal *presence to* all reality. When we talk about God we talk about the *Thou* who relates at every level to all reality, for whom there is only an 'I-Thou' and no 'I-It', and whose relationship keeps it in being. Thus this relationship, a '*spiritual*' relationship of love, is truly causal. At the same time because it describes the relation between the universe and a God who is not a member of this universe it cannot in any obvious sense be a subject of scientific investigation for science is limited to this universe. It is true that belief in providence makes empirical claims, as Langford insists, but these can only be assessed by *theological* science.[41] The 'intelligibility to be grasped' in this case is faith in the God who has revealed himself measured against the totality of human experience. This means that such faith is open to disconfirmation. The world might be, as many have claimed, the kind of place which makes it quite incredible to believe in any form of providence at all. It is this possibility which we have now to try and assess.

3

Providence and Evil

The attempt to reconcile the infinite benevolence, justice and power of God with our experience of this world, wrote J.S.Mill, 'not only involves absolute contradiction in an intellectual point of view but exhibits the revolting spectacle of a jesuitical defence of moral enormities'.[1] Can we continue to believe in providence without either justifying evil, or minimizing its reality, and at the same time continuing to affirm that 'God is light and in him there is no darkness at all' (I John 1.5)? In attempting to respond to this question we shall follow Leibniz' classification of evil into three types, physical, moral and metaphysical.

Pain, suffering and death

The question of the reason for pain and suffering is rarely posed as such in the Christian scriptures, although Genesis 3 preserves reflection from a very early period on the suffering inherent in human life. That story passes from the disobedience to God's command to the consequences which ensue: the subjection of woman to man, the pain of childbirth, and the toil and labour involved in producing food. These things are regarded not so much as a punishment for sin as a reflection on the consequences of human alienation from God. A connection between sin and suffering is, however, assumed from earliest times, originating, perhaps, in the idea of breach of taboo (e.g.I Sam.14). The experience of the exile led to the challenging of this connection and the affirmation that individuals would suffer for their own sin (Ezek. 18). This in turn seems to have provoked both the intense questioning of Job, who could not conceive how God could be just and loving in a world marked by overwhelming personal suffering, and the scepticism of Ecclesiastes, who concluded that God's rule was fundamentally arbitrary. Job puts a question against the view, which we otherwise find in every part of the tradition, that suffering is part of the divine education. This view, which represents an attempt to interpret all aspects of experience, no matter how dreadful, as manifestations of God's lordship, stands in some tension with the conviction that in his deepest and most inward essence God is Saviour. 'Salvation' includes peace, freedom, and physical well being – the opposite of everything which brings death. As the living God YHWH is no friend of anything which diminishes life. With the exception of Ecclesiastes the scriptures of Israel and church nowhere teach resignation. Bodily illnesses are not to be endured but resisted and God is besought for deliverance from them (cf.II Kings 20). It is because Jesus stands in this tradition that he comes not simply teaching and preaching but healing the sick and raising the dead. The question he puts to his opponents is: 'Is it lawful on the sabbath to do good or to do evil, to save life or to kill?' (Mark 3.4). He comes to 'save life' by restoring human wholeness in every dimension, physical and spiritual. The completion of his work, as the gospels and as Paul view it, is the resurrection in which in his own person he defeats death as a promise for the rest of the human race. Death, too, for this tradition is never 'Sister Death' or 'friendly death' but 'the last enemy'. If, in view of the resurrection, we do not die as those 'without hope', all the same this no more encourages us to embrace death with open arms than Christ did.

In contrast to this scriptural tradition the theologians of the church have attempted to understand pain and suffering more positively as falling within a providential scheme. Both Augustine and Aquinas argue, following Plato, that shadow is needed to appreciate the light, pain to alert us to the joy of full health, and suffering to appreciate happiness. The gross form of this position was parodied by Voltaire in *Candide*, and falls under Mill's condemnation. Barth, more sensitively, tried to reinterpret this theme by speaking of some forms of decay, ugliness and death as the 'Shadowside' of creation. These things are not necessarily evil in themselves, he said, but also praise the Creator and Lord in their own way, and were heard to do so by Mozart. Since Christ himself took this element upon himself in becoming flesh its essential goodness is revealed, even though its proximity to nothingness is apparent. Barth felt that this 'shadowside' should not be confused with the evil he called 'nothingness'. In that case,

> nothingness suddenly becomes a something which is ultimately innocuous, and even salutary. Real sin can then be regarded as a venial error and mistake, a temporary retardation, and comprendre c'est pardonner. Real evil can then be interpreted as transitory and not intolerable perfection, and real death as 'rest in God'. The devil can then be denied or described as the last candidate for a salvation which is due to him by reason of a general apokatastasis. Nothingness can then be tidily 'demythologized', although in actual fact what is in question is not real nothingness, but only the misconceived negative side of creation, which is not null *in re* . . . While we look in the wrong direction, and there hope to hear ultimate harmonies and accomplish ultimate syntheses, they are not taken seriously in their reality.[2]

The difficulty with this important and necessary distinction is in fixing what is shadow and what belongs to the realm of nothingness. Towards the end of his life Barth had a long series of illnesses and wrote to a former student,

> Somewhere within me there lives a bacillus with the name *proteus mirabilis*, which has an inclination to enter my kidneys – which would then be my finish. I am certain that this monstrosity does not belong to God's good creation but rather has first come in as a result of the Fall. It has in common with sin and with the demons that it cannot be simply done away with but can only be just despised, combatted and suppressed.[3]

'Many a true word', we may add, as there are clearly many forms of pain and suffering which to the victim cannot be part of God's good creation, but must be an aspect of nothingness.

Another response to the facts of pain and suffering is to take up the biblical idea that they form part of God's education of the human race. Many theologians in the present century have taken up in one way or another what John Hick called the 'Irenaean theodicy',[4] the view that creation as it is is the only kind of environment which can produce free and loving beings. Thus H.H.Farmer described providence as 'the adequacy of God's wisdom and power to the task with which he has charged himself', namely, 'to fashion men through freedom into sonship to himself and brotherhood to one another or . . . to build . . . a kingdom of love'.[5] This 'Irenaean' view of God's action in history understands the inequalities of life as providing 'the major opportunities for the generous bearing of one another's burdens without which love cannot be manifested, and a fellowship which is more than a superficial camaraderie, achieved'.[6] Clearly, if the political implications of this were followed up it would mean extremely bad news for the poor.

A more recent account of this approach is Andrew Elphinstone's *Freedom, Suffering and Love*, a book written against the background of the author's chronic ill health, and published posthumously. He begins from the facts of evolution, regarding aggression on the one hand and vulnerability to pain on the other as the most ancient and fundamental part of human experience. It is pain, or the possibility of pain, which grounds our sensitivity. Like Farmer he conceives the purpose of creation to be that beings may evolve who respond to God's love and participate meaningfully in the divine life. From this point his argument develops in five steps. First he argues that love cannot be commanded into existence, and therefore demands freedom. Freedom (the next step) requires growth for something which was ready made would neither be free nor able to respond. Growth requires pain, as a warning device, as an incentive to development, but more importantly as 'a fundamental prerequisite for the forming of relationships invested with sensitivity and awareness of values termed human'.[7] This necessity for pain entails the fact that it may be misused, that it may 'wear the face of sin, wielding the weapons of provocation and self aggrandisement, and issuing in disturbance, damage and destruction, enmity and revenge'. This, however, is not a failure in the divine plan but is necessary to its consummation. It is this 'illegitimate' side of pain which is 'pressed into service to authenticate and perfect love'.

No love is truly love until it has been proved capable of standing undeterred at the prospect or actuality of pain inflicted by another's disaffection. The apex of the divine wisdom is perceived in the fact that the pains and travails which are inseparable from our growth as persons are capable of being redesigned into the means of drawing forth a quality of love which would not, without those pains, come into being . . . It is the means of calling forth love at a more than natural, in other words supernatural level, a love which can disregard the pain experienced and can continue to go out undiminished towards the perpetrator. That love which seeks to remain undeterred and undiminished in face of pain is none other than the principal ingredient of forgiveness. Forgiveness is the crowning achievement of love both in God and man.[8]

As with Barth's account of the 'shadowside' there are elements here which are indispensable to any account of providence. The idea that the world is 'the arena of humankind's making' above all else, so that we are not to look for a world where all are blissfully happy all the time. On the other hand the possibility that sin and pain may have been *designed* to make forgiveness possible smacks of Mill's 'moral enormities'. Is it really the case that love is not 'truly love' until tested by another's disaffection? Like the 'O felix culpa' of the Easter Exultet, Elphinstone's argument comes perilously near to justifying the sin without which love would not be perfect. But in that case this is not the sin which is opposed and rejected by God. Again, this acceptance of the necessity of pain which, were it abolished would have to be re-invented seems a far cry from the biblical view that pain and suffering are things from which we need deliverance. Even the claim that 'pain in itself is neutral' is doubtful, as there is pain which is not inflicted by sin which can still humiliate and break people. If pain, why so much, so cruel, so unendurable, and so unevenly distributed? There are two responses we can make to this question (apart from that of atheism). One is to postulate some kind of 'fall' or defection from God on the part of the whole of creation. Regarding all forms of reality as capable of some level of response to God, process theology then understands 'natural evil' as a failure to respond to the divine persuasion. Proteus mirabilis and the Lisbon earthquake alike are the product of resistance to God. Giving a cautious welcome to this view Paul Fiddes feels that some overall vision both of the responsiveness and of the resistance of the whole of creation to God is necessary for a doctrine of creative evolution, for a proper theodicy and for the idea that God suffers conflict with a non-being alien to him. We must think of nature 'as generating something strange to God if we are to say he suffers within it.'[9] Pan-mentalism argues from analogy with human experience, and points to the interaction of all levels of being. Ironically process thought here follows a procedure analogous to that of thoroughgoing materialism and falls prey to the reductionist fallacy, failing to respect the fact that whilst higher levels of being need lower levels to explain them they cannot themselves be reduced downward.

A second response, therefore, is to appeal to the importance of chance in universal process. A world with all the properties necessary to fulfil God's purposes, argues Bartholomew, could not avoid being one in which accidents happen, and this would account for the unequal distribution of pain in every sense. Then we have to understand one of the purposes of the incarnation as demonstrating the difference between God's true nature and the accidental and harmful accompaniments of creation.[10] There could not be real freedom without this kind of chance and the suffering which comes with it is simply the price we have to pay for love and for freedom. We then have the unanswerable question whether the price is not too high, a question which could only be answered at the end of history if at all.

Sin

The Jewish and Christian tradition has always seen the heart of the problem of evil not in pain and suffering, as Buddhism does, but in sin. How does sin find a place in the good creation of the good God? There are three types of answer to this question. The first of these follows Paul and his rabbinic teachers in speaking of a 'Fall'. When Genesis 3 is read in this way it becomes a story of human failure to trust in God and his promises, of willed rejection and refusal of the divine command. Von Rad emphasizes the significance of the fact that sin is located in the area of human hubris rather than in a plunge into moral evil.[11] This is to follow Augustine in understanding pride, the human desire to be 'as

God', as the fundamental human sin. Pride is the obverse of idolatry, in which the creature refuses God in his humility and worships an arrogant and powerful god made in his own image. 'Claiming to be wise, they became fools . . . they exchanged the truth about God for a lie and worshipped and served the creature rather than the Creator' (Rom.1.22,25). Both pride and idolatry are rooted in unbelief and this, for the Jewish and Christian tradition in general, is the essence of sin. 'Whatsoever is not of faith is sin' (Rom.14.23). This account of sin and its origin focusses on human responsibility. Sin is a conscious choice *for* idols and *against* the living God. Some, such as Augustine, add that some of the angels 'fell' from God in the same way and are active in fomenting human sin. In both cases sin is something which cannot be excused but may be forgiven, and it is the death of Christ which makes this possible.

A second, very different, approach to sin begins with Schleiermacher and presupposes either an evolutionary or developmental view of human history. Schleiermacher begins from the fact that the purpose of creation is to provide an environment for the emergence of human 'God consciousness'. Sin is the term we use for any arrestment of the disposition to God consciousness due to the 'independence of the sensuous functions' whereby 'the spirit is obstructed in its actions by the flesh'.[12] The basic cause of sin is therefore man's being as a creature organic to the animal kingdom, whose consciousness is accordingly focussed on the natural environment. Were the God consciousness not obscured. Schleiermacher argued, then suffering, pain, disease and even death would not be experienced as evil but simply as an unavoidable imperfection.

The most controversial aspect of this teaching is that because redemption only begins to operate after sin has attained to a certain degree 'we need have no misgivings in saying that God is also the Author of sin'.[13] God has ordained that the continually imperfect triumph of the spirit should become sin in us and he is therefore the author of sin only as he negates it, solely as the consciousness of sin is the cause of our displeasure at ourselves which thus causes us to seek redemption. The gradual and imperfect unfolding of the power of the God consciousness which gives rise to sin is 'one of the necessary conditions of the human stage of existence'.

From the very beginning it was especially this aspect of Schleiermacher's work which was singled out for attack, and Barth speaks of it as a 'theological catastrophe of the first order'. Schleiermacher grants that sin has no ground in the divine causality, but then goes on to say that it was ordained as that which makes redemption necessary. But in that case grace is simply the antithesis of sin, conditioned by it and not known without it. Barth maintained, by contrast, that the only relation between sin and grace was one of 'real conflict' in which there can be no mediation. Sin is culpable and God himself wishes to negate it.

A contemporary, post Darwinian, account of sin which resembles Schleiermacher's is that of the Uruguayan liberation theologian Juan Segundo. Like Elphinstone he begins from the fact that 'man is not a finished, ready made concept'. 'The word *"man"* designates a painfully slow process whereby the evolution of the animal kingdom gradually gives rise to a being we are willing to call "man" only in a certain sense and with great difficulty.'[14] To speak of 'human beings' is to speak of one animal species which is 'being hominized'. But how can the 'immobilist' language of freely chosen sin and consequent guilt apply to such a creature? Moral conscience is still emerging from the tangle of instincts and determinisms which are humankind's evolutionary base and so we have to understand sin in evolutionary terms. Evolution is effected by displacing energy, concentrating it, drawing it away from one function and putting it to another. The law of entropy, that energy is always conserved but also degraded in the process, applies here as elsewhere. Evolution, then, only proceeds by overcoming entropy. On the one hand there is the production of more complex and potent concentrations of energy which we see in evolution; on the other hand the statistically greater tendency toward the degeneration of energy which, by itself, would make evolution impossible. 'All sin is anti-evolutionary' – a statement H. R. Mackintosh had made sixty years before Segundo.[15] For Segundo the Johannine 'world' terminology speaks of a frozen and therefore anti-evolutionary outlook. It is conservative ideology, 'the recourse to the easy way out that precludes richer human syntheses', which is sin, though without revelation it is not known to be so. Like Schleiermacher Segundo ascribes a certain positive role to sin. Because 'sin' is a name for forces which derive from our evolutionary heritage, it is the very base and foundation for the unity of the human species and for our solidarity with the universe. It is the base of our liberty which puts up resistance to that liberty. It is the world that makes the Incarnation possible and then tries to suffocate it. It is the flesh of society that needs redemption and flees from it.[16]

Segundo speaks of sin in much the same terms Elphinstone had used of pain. For the one 'sin' and for the other 'pain' is our 'evolutionary base'. Both maintain that evolution shows up earlier ways of thinking as 'immobilist' – based on mythological conceptions of creation which offer existential insights but which must be corrected by the awareness of the slow growth of life from one original 'material' explosion.

Segundo speaks of positive and negative 'vectors' in evolutionary process – love versus egotism, grace versus sin, difficult syntheses versus facile syntheses, liberty versus law, minority lines of conduct versus majority – which are not hostile but 'indispensable and complementary, each in its own way'.[17] God works *with* the sin of human beings – not just in spite of it. And thus, like Schleiermacher, Segundo ends up by justifying sin in a way which hardly squares with the biblical emphasis on God's opposition to it and also, incidentally, undercuts the essential factor of human responsibility. Segundo's position is strange for a theologian of liberation since oppression must be 'indispensable and complementary' to liberation.

A third view of sin argues that we can trace sin neither to pride nor to our evolutionary base because sin is something radically unintelligible. This takes us to the third section, 'metaphysical' evil.

Evil

What Leibniz called 'metaphysical evil' has been very variously referred to as 'the principalities and powers', 'Satan', or 'Das Nichtige' – Nothingness. These names and phrases denote a force of evil which may find expression in human sin but which goes beyond this and which is primarily the opponent of God rather than of human beings. How are we to account for the virulence and reality of evil? Augustine addressed this question in asking why completely good creatures should fall. On one level he simply denied an explanation:

> If you try to find the efficient cause of this evil choice, there is none to be found . . . It is not a matter of efficiency, but of deficiency; the evil will itself is not effective but defective. For to defect from him who is the Supreme Existence, to something of less reality, this is to begin to have an evil will. To try to discover the causes of such defection – deficient, not efficient causes – is like trying to see darkness or to hear silence.[18]

At the same time the creature's falling away from its true being 'is due to its creation out of nothing'.[19] To an extent, therefore, mutability is the root of the problem, sheer creatureliness. Augustine shares the Neo-Platonic view that there are degrees of reality and goodness, at the apex of which is God. Everything is created good, but not everything is created equal. When goodness, and therefore reality, is diminished, there is evil. Evil is thus parasitic on good and cannot exist without it as a purely evil thing cannot exist at all.

This conception of evil enabled Augustine both to affirm the sole ultimate power of God and the fundamental goodness of creation. Whilst he had a vivid sense of human bondage to sin however, it is doubtful whether the 'privation of good' language enables him to do justice to the nature of evil as that which *opposes* God. His use of what John Hick calls the 'principle of plenitude' – the argument that more things are necessarily better than fewer, even if they are cancer cells or tsetse fly – and of the 'aesthetic theme', according to which evils constitute the necessary shading which help us to appreciate the beauty of creation, both underline this suspicion.

Hick remarks that 'every position that maintains the perfect goodness of God is bound either to let go the absolute divine power and freedom, or else to hold that evil exists ultimately within God's good purpose'.[20] This is not quite an accurate statement of the *privatio boni* argument according to which evil is a *defection* from God's good purpose, but in any case Barth refuses this simplified option. Picking up a strand of Augustinian (neo Platonic) vocabulary Barth spoke of evil as 'Das Nichtige', 'Nothingness', but gave this a quite different content to the neo-Platonic 'inclining towards non existence'. Barth's suggestion is that radical evil stems from God's refusal, what he said 'No' to when he created the universe:

> Even on his left hand the activity of God is not in vain. He does not act for nothing. His rejection, opposition, negation and dismissal are powerful and effective like all his works because they, too, are grounded in himself, in the freedom and wisdom of his election. That which God renounces and abandons in virtue of his decision is not merely nothing. It is nothingness, and as such has its own being, albeit malignant and perverse. A real dimension is disclosed, and existence and form are given to a reality *sui generis*, in the fact that God is wholly and utterly not the Creator in this respect. Nothingness is that which God does not will. It lives only by the fact that it is that which God does not will. But it does live by this fact. For not only what God wills, but what he does not will is potent and must have a real correspondence. What really corresponds to that which God does not will is nothingness.[21]

The biggest problem with this account is not its 'naive mythology' but the fact that it seems to suggest that God had no choice but to admit evil into his creation. As Hick observes the theory suggests the paradox that God cannot prevent the presence and operation of evil, yet once evil arises he can and does combat and exterminate it.[22] The origin of this paradox probably lies in Barth's insistence on God's omnipotence.

Taking up Barth's terminology John Cowburn has strongly opposed any concept of evil as somehow 'all for the good'. There is evil which is deliberate wickedness and which God opposes with his whole being. He rejects William Temple's statement that it is incredible that a human being ever chose evil knowing it to be evil *for them* – a view which goes back to Augustine. On the contrary, as the psalmist says, there are those who 'love evil more than good, and lying more than speaking the truth' (Ps.52.3).[23] Human beings can rejoice and gloat in evil. Hatred is not simply lack of love, nor evil lack of perfection, but they have their own vicious dynamic. Just as there can be a consciously willed choice for the good, so may there be for evil. This choice, he insists, is inexplicable and he agrees with Brunner that 'all attempts to explain evil end by explaining it away; they end by denying the fact of evil altogether'.[24] At the same time he finds the essence of positive evil not, as Augustine did, in self love, but in self hatred, and this suggests a way of understanding the Fall and Nothingness.

Cowburn draws freely on world literature to illustrate that the evil which is rooted in self hatred amounts to a kind of vertigo, a headlong flight from the true, good and beautiful. The heart of its intent is *annihilation*. Hatred of self finds expression in the will to destroy, corrupt or deface all those things which show the self how detestable it is. This means that the degree of hatred and wickedness may be proportionate to the goodness and love encountered. In a celebrated phrase Coleridge spoke of Iago's hatred of Othello as 'motiveless malignity' but in fact this hatred is called forth by Othello's goodness, simplicity and trust. Hatred is a refusal of love and this refusal is not measured but the slip off the cliff edge which can hurl us into the abyss. The language of 'falling' thus draws attention to a genuine characteristic of human evil. Evil is not 'rational' in the sense of being a reaction to a wrong done. It is a reaction to goodness: just so does John understand evil in his gospel, characterizing it in terms of darkness and blindness.

If this is a true account of human experience then this helps also to understand the flight from God. It is not, as Barth suggests, that what God refuses 'somehow or other' has its own malign existence but that God's being as love, simply because it is love, can call forth the vertiginous flight of evil. For there to be love, as Elphinstone rightly says, there must be freedom to accept or refuse, but refusal is a headlong fall. Could God have made creatures which were not liable to this fall? The answer seems to be – not if he wanted the free response of love. Evil and hatred are in no sense instrumental to God's purpose but the deepest secret of God's providence is to turn evil against itself and make it work for good, and of this work of subversion the cross is a sign.

Antony Flew dubbed this kind of response the 'Free Will Defence', and his attack on it engendered a long debate.[25] The heart of his contention was that there is no contradiction in saying that God might have created people who always chose rightly. But then, it was argued, if creatures can only do what is right, they cannot do it freely. The discussion is sterile because it has been misconceived. It is not a freewill defence but a 'Logic of love' defence. The purpose of creation was the solicitation of love, and since love can only be free the possibility of refusal and rejection were necessarily entailed in such a creation. Because refusal brings about self hatred, and self hatred the will to destroy all that is good, such a refusal amounts to a 'fall' into 'nothingness', chaos and destruction.

Freedom and love, which together constitute 'grace', are at the heart both of the possibility of pain, sin and evil, and of the response to this. The question of inequality is bound up with this in a world where purpose works through chance, and chance is embraced by purpose. It is the reality of chance which makes it seem that we exist as flies to the wanton gods. But, in the first place, it is precisely this chance which is the instrument of the Creator who gives and seeks love, and secondly, God is not at the mercy of 'the law of large numbers'. In and through the free reign of chance he accomplishes his purpose. How this can be affirmed is what doctrine of providence seeks to discern.

4

Knowledge, Power and Providence

No comfort is to be derived, wrote Bertrand Russell, from the supposition that this very unpleasing universe was manufactured of set purpose.

> If indeed the world in which we live has been produced in accordance with a Plan, we shall have to reckon Nero a saint in comparison with the Author of that Plan. Fortunately however, the evidence of Divine Purpose is non existent . . . We are therefore spared the necessity for that attitude of impotent hatred which every brave and humane man would otherwise be called upon to adopt towards the Almighty Tyrant.[1]

Accounts of providence in terms of the actions of this divine Tyrant may be found to lie in a set of assumptions about God's knowledge and power, not derived from scripture but in the light of which the scriptures were read. Countless scriptural passages could be proof texted and used to confirm a view of God which was appealing on other grounds. At the root of much Western theologizing lies the gut reaction of Parmenides and Plato to the problem of transcience. They looked at a world where youth grew pale and spectre thin and died and could not accept that it was final. In his cosmology Plato begins by distinguishing that which always is and never becomes from that which is always becoming and never is. The former is the object of rational knowledge and is always eternally the same, the other the object of opinion and irrational sensation and is not fully real (*Timaeus*

29). It followed that 'the One', or what Christian theologians later called God, belonged to the realm of being and not becoming. Only such a Being could offer hope for those condemned to the nightmare of decay. An existential necessity determines the metaphysical adequacy of the idea of God. To be God must be to be beyond the limits of becoming, of chance and decay. Once this fundamental assumption was granted all sorts of other assumptions followed, particularly about God's *knowledge* and *power*. We find assumptions about the former worked out, for instance, in Augustine's *De Trinitate* and later quarried and systematized by Aquinas.[2] The argument goes as follows: it is taken as an axiom that a truly supreme Being must be omniscient; but God's knowledge is coterminous with his causality. 'He does not know (his creatures) because they are, but they are because he knows them . . . He created because he knew.'[3] Therefore God both foreknows and causes both all that is and all events, including contingent ones, as we have seen. Augustine sought to reconcile these views with human freewill by appealing to God's eternity, the fact that God comprehends all things in 'a stable and eternal present'.[4] God exists in a never ending present which embraces all created happening. God's knowledge, then, could best be understood on the analogy of memory. Just as a person's remembering something does not make the event they remember necessary, so neither does God's foreknowing an event make it necessary. Tackling the same difficulty Boethius appealed to the analogy of a sign which shows that to which it points without producing it. In the same way, he argues, God knows what will come to pass but his knowing does not cause it to happen.[5] However, the triple identification of predestination, foreknowledge and grace which we find, for instance in Augustine's writing on predestination,[6] certainly implies that omniscience is omni-causality. When this is the case Mill's 'jesuitical defence of moral enormities' is more or less unavoidable.

A second set of assumptions attend discussions of God's power. The mutability of creatures results from their essential powerlessness. By contrast it is the 'common confession', as Aquinas puts it, that God is Almighty, though he qualifies this by saying that God's power is not power to do anything whatsoever, but power to do what is logically possible. God cannot undo the past or make a person a donkey for instance.[7]

No one has emphasized the omnipotence of God more strongly than Karl Barth who insists that God is not 'much in much' but 'all in all'. His operation is as sovereign as Calvinist teaching describes it: 'In the strictest sense it is predestinating.'[8] Barth is fond of the image of God as the supreme chess master who will never be outplayed by his opponents: though the opponent may not know it the checkmate is already decided in advance.[9] God is both Plan and Planner and what he has decided for the creature is never in any sense limited or even conditioned by the creature. No limits must be set to the omnipotence of God. To propose such limits is to contend for 'the greatest possible evil that could befall the creature as such'.[10] This insistence on God's omnipotence is qualified in two ways. First, we live under the *fatherly* lordship of God, who rules in a 'kind, friendly and loving way'. God's omnipotence is not power in itself, which would simply be another name for evil, but personal power. But then secondly when we ask whether God's will is done 'completely, unconditionally and irresistibly' in, for instance, Auschwitz, we find that, uniquely in Christian theology, Barth does not have *one* statement of providence but *two*. After his exposition of the omnipotence of God's fatherly lordship in creaturely occurrence he starts the fiftieth paragraph of the *Dogmatics*:

> There is in world occurrence an element, indeed an entire sinister system of elements, which is not comprehended by God's providence in the same sense thus far described, and which is not therefore preserved, accompanied, nor ruled by the almighty action of God like creaturely occurrence . . . *Thus the whole doctrine of God's providence must be investigated afresh.*[11]

Barth reconciles this with his earlier statements about God's will being done in all occurrence through the concept of 'permission', an idea which goes back to Origen. God can be said to 'will' evil in so far as he gives it space, position and function. He wills it 'as he denies it his authorship, as he refuses it any standing before him or right or blessing or promise, as he places it under his prohibition and curse and treats it as that from which he wishes to redeem and liberate his creation'.[12] Barth is forced to this position partly by his ferocious opposition to any autonomy on the part of the creature. Molinism, a seventeenth-century Jesuit view which proposed that there was an area where human beings could co-operate or refuse to co-operate with God, is characterized as a 'heathen atavism'. The idea of autonomy implies that creatures may condition God and 'the creature which conditions God is no longer God's creature, and the God who is conditioned by the creature is no longer God'.[13] Barth agrees with the Thomists that 'the doctrine of creaturely freedom as a limitation of God's omnicausality and omnipotence, and therefore a denial of his sovereignty, involves an attack on his deity and makes prayer, if not impossible, at least superfluous'.[14]

Assumptions such as these about God's knowledge and power have constituted the ground rules for reflection on providence since at least the time of Augustine. They appeal to the logic of an infinite being, but, if it is part of the function of revelation to tell us what we cannot tell ourselves then should we not be warned off a picture of God which appears in many respects to be a Freudian projection of our own sense of impotence or a reaction to the tragic element of mutability? These views of God's knowledge and power can certainly appeal to scripture, by way of proof texts, but can they do so legitimately? The attempt to develop a specifically Christian doctrine of providence has to begin with this question.

Knowledge and wisdom

> The Lord is a God of knowledge
> and by him acts are weighed (I Sam.2.3).

Texts which can be quarried to show that God must be omniscient abound in the Old Testament yet we have to ask what it is these texts are truly wanting to tell us. Nowhere do we find an abstract insistence on the importance of God's omniscience as such. Rather, a number of aspects of God's knowledge are emphasized. There is, for instance, frequent emphasis on the *depth* of God's knowledge:

> O Lord thou hast searched me and known me!
> Thou knowest when I sit down and when I rise up;
> thou discernest my thoughts from afar . . . (Ps.139.1f).

There is sometimes emphasis on the *extent* of God's knowledge as opposed to human knowledge. Whereas human beings cannot find the way to wisdom,

> God understands the way to it, and he knows its place.
> For he looks to the ends of the earth,
> and sees everything under the heavens (Job 28.23-4).

For Second Isaiah it is partly *knowledge of the future* which marks God off from the idols:

> Thus says the Lord, the King of Israel . . .
> I am the first and I am the last;
> beside me there is no god . . . . . .
> Who has announced from of old the things to
> come?
> Let them tell us what is yet to be (Isa. 44.6f.).

Frequent references to God's plan, purpose or promise also imply that God knows the future. 'Before I formed you in the womb I knew you', says God to Jeremiah; 'before you were born I consecrated you; I appointed you a prophet to the nations' (Jer. 1.5). God's knowledge of the future seems to be conveyed in the New Testament by the use of the particle *dei*, 'it is necessary', or 'must'. The so called passion predictions all say that the Son of Man 'must' suffer as foretold by the scriptures (Mark 8.31 and parallels). Luke emphasizes this even more strongly. In the first of his speeches in Jerusalem Peter says: 'this Jesus, delivered up *according to the definite plan and foreknowledge of God*, you crucified and killed' (Acts 2.23). Matthew understands the whole of Jesus' story in terms of the fulfilment of prophecy and Paul too says that what happened in Christ was that which God 'promised beforehand through his prophets in the holy scriptures' (Rom. 1.2).

Read out of context, as they are when they are proof texted, these ideas can easily be felt to describe what Farmer calls 'the unspeakably sterile and depressing spectacle of omniscience playing an everlasting game of patience with itself, all possible combinations of the cards being already known by heart'.[15] Fortunately there are at least three reasons why we cannot in fact read them in this way. First, as Eichrodt put it, 'The whole ethical exhortation of the prophets is based on the conviction that decision is placed in the hands of men. But the Law too, setting before men the choice of life and death, rests on this presupposition.'[16] It is actually not the case that the overwhelming impression conveyed by scripture is of human beings acting out parts already scripted for them. On the contrary, there is human action, such as David's adultery, or Jezebel's assassination of Naboth, and God's reaction. There is call and response, on both sides. Human beings call, and God responds; God calls, and people respond. The same assumptions about the importance of human choice lie behind both Jesus' teaching on discipleship and the question of responsibility for his betrayal and death. The strong affirmations of necessity which the gospels contain express the feeling that given that God is who he is, and given the way in which human beings behave, things have to happen in this way. The 'must' of the passion narratives is an expression of the logic of sin and grace. The story of the risen Jesus interpreting to the despairing disciples 'in all the scriptures the things concerning himself' (Luke 24.27) so that at last the inner meaning of the scriptures is opened to them 'and their eyes were opened and they recognized him' is the paradigm of this moment of insight. It is insight into the logic of love which the 'must' expresses.

Secondly, the scriptures do not speak with one voice but represent a dialogue, a struggle for the truth. This is represented in microcosm by the book of Job which must be understood, in fact, as a protest against Russell's 'Almighty Tyrant'. True, the book ends with Job silenced and the Almighty emphasizing the feebleness of human knowledge when compared with the divine, exactly the position the friends have advocated. In the Dialogue on the other hand Job protests against such a God and puts his faith in quite a different picture of him. In words reminiscent of Hosea he appeals to God as a tender father:

> Thou wouldest call, and I would answer thee; thou wouldest long for the work of thy hands. For then thou wouldest number my steps, thou wouldest not keep watch over my sin; my transgression would be sealed up in a bag, and thou wouldest cover over my iniquity (14.15-17).

The climax of the book of Job is not the familiar passage where

Job affirms faith in his 'redeemer' but the beautiful picture of his dialogue with God:

> Oh, that I knew where I might find him,
> that I might come even to his seat!
> I would lay my case before him
> and fill my mouth with arguments.
> I would learn that he would answer me,
> and understand what he would say to me.
> *Would he contend with me in the greatness of*
> *his power? No; he would give heed to me.*
> *There an upright man could reason with*
> *him, and I should be acquitted for ever by*
> *my judge* (23.3-7).

Barth considered Job to be a 'type' of Christ, the True Witness, in that he held on to God throughout his sufferings, which we can accept if we understand an appeal 'from God against God', where the 'God' appealed against is the projection of human fantasies of omnipotence. Equally, however, Job could be considered the 'type' of the justified sinner, who can approach God with confidence knowing that God will not 'contend with him in the greatness of his power'. Earlier Job has accused the tyrant God of 'putting him in the wrong'. What he sought was what lies at the heart of Paul's gospel, the picture of God putting the sinner in the right. If Job is at all a type of Christ it is surely as the one who refuses to believe in the Almighty Tyrant and who, in the face of the tyranny of chance, continues to believe in the God of reason and mercy, the God who, in Jesus, suffers alongside his creatures. The various writings of the Bible represent a long and complex struggle for the truth, and the truth towards which they are moving is summed up in the picture of Jesus. In this struggle quite different perceptions contend for dominance, and it is for this reason that it cannot be quarried for proof texts but must be 'listened in to', as we listen in to a dialogue.

Thirdly at no point is the concern of the Bible with knowledge as such. That God knows absolutely everything is often an implicit assumption but it is not something that the biblical writers are concerned to establish. The prophets, for instance, are concerned with God's promises rather than predictions of the future. Their exhortation has no meaning if God cannot change his mind, and they saw his promises fulfilled in unexpected ways. More importantly knowledge is an adjunct of wisdom, and not the other way round. Concluding his argument about Israel and the Gentiles Paul exclaims: 'For God has consigned all to disobedience that he might have mercy on all. O the depths of the riches and wisdom and knowledge of God!' (Rom. 11.32). 'Knowledge' here is obviously only another way of talking of wisdom: God's plan for the salvation of all people does not hang on his omniscience. The distinction between knowledge on the one hand, which is a source and means of power, and wisdom on the other, which includes the just and right use of knowledge, is familiar. This distinction is implicit in the common sense wisdom of ancient Israel, which was later theologized in a most significant way when Wisdom was personified and portrayed as the consort of God and mediatrix of creation (Prov. 8; Ecclus. 1). This development proved of great significance to Jesus and the writers of the New Testament. Jesus taught using the language of Wisdom, bidding people not to be 'foolish' (Matt. 7.27), comparing his wisdom to that of Solomon (Matt. 12.42), inviting the poor to come to him in the language of Wisdom (cf. Matt. 11.25f. and Ecclus. 6.18f.;51.23f.) and appealing to the wisdom which is 'justified by her deeds' (Matt. 11.19). It is therefore no surprise that the risen and glorified Christ is identified with personified Wisdom both by John, whose Prologue echoes the great Wisdom hymns of Proverbs 8 and Wisdom 7, and by Paul for whom Jesus fulfils the function of Wisdom as mediator of creation (Col. 1.15f.).

All of this points us to the priority of the concept of Wisdom in understanding God. It is in the crucified Christ that 'all the treasures of wisdom and knowledge are hid' (Col. 2.3), and 'the unsearchable riches of Christ' are 'the manifold wisdom of God' (Eph. 3.10). It is a wisdom which addresses the lowly (Matt. 11.25f.) and, like the promised Messiah of Isaiah 11, on whom the spirit of wisdom and understanding rests, 'judges the poor with righteousness and decides with equity for the meek of the earth'. It is this which is the focus of the biblical writings, and not a God who terrifies through omniscience. This wisdom is endlessly creative, fertile, surprising, as Paul says – its depth compasses every depth of the created universe. Whilst God's knowledge of the future is certainly affirmed the emphasis is in fact on the divine *purpose*, a purpose which is liberative and seeks human fullness. To give it the most pointed expression, Jesus is the wisdom of God and thus wisdom is focussed in the cross. On the cross we learn what God's wisdom, which is to say his providential rule, really amounts to. It amounts to taking the self-hatred of the human race and meeting it with forgiveness, in so doing starting a new chapter of the human story. Belief in God's providence involves faith and hope that God's purpose will prevail over every negative force – not that the details of the victory are worked out to the minutest detail. It may be that the etymology of 'providence' in the Latin *provideo*, 'to see to beforehand' or 'to make provision for' points to God's foreseeing of all things. But we must not be misled by this. *Providence is God's wisdom in action, and what that means is seen in Christ*. It is the implications of that which a Christian doctrine of providence needs to explore.

Redefining power

> I form light and create darkness,
> I make weal and create woe,
> I am the Lord, who do all these
> things (Isa. 45.7).

As with knowledge, so with power: there are endless texts which can be appealed to to support belief in God's omnipotence. In his controversy with the Pelagians Augustine appealed over and over again to the texts about God hardening Pharaoh's heart, and to the metaphor of the pot and the potter used by Paul in Romans. These texts became classical for the discussion of providence but they did so precisely because the proof texting method was adopted, and the direction of the argument in scripture as a whole was not discerned.

As we have seen talk about providence from a biblical perspective is talk about God's rule or sovereignty. Everything that we read in the Old Testament, said Ludwig Köhler, however rich in content and significance it may be, 'is but the corollary of the statement "God is Lord"'.[17] But is not the 'Lord' of the Old

Testament the God of Battles, given to annihilating his enemies? Charles Raven felt that people brought up in Sunday School on stories of Jael and Samuel would always be encouraged to be warmongers.[18] Certainly there are themes from the Canaanite cult such as we find in Ps.29 which glorify the God who makes the oaks whirl, a sort of celestial King Kong, and there are war psalms like the Song of Miriam in Exodus 15 which speak of God 'sending forth his fury' and 'consuming his enemies like stubble', more a celestial Rambo. If we take the overall drift of the Old Testament, however, the much maligned 'canonical sense', then what emerges is a *redefinition* of sovereignty. Whilst Isaiah can still speak of God 'sifting the nations with the sieve of destruction' (Isa. 30.27-8) Hosea emphasizes that God's anger is only 'for a moment':

> My heart recoils within me,
> My compassion grows warm and tender.
> I will not execute my fierce anger;
> I will not again destroy Ephraim;
> for I am God and not man,
> the Holy One in your midst,
> and I will not come to
> destroy (Hos. 11.8–9).

The most decisive instance of re-interpretation is the way the analogy of royal power is inverted. To image God as a king was natural in a monarchical society. According to royal ideology the king had been the 'servant' of YHWH but this ideology functioned to mask a ruthless and illegitimate exercise of power. The vision of the servant which emerged during the exile turned all this on its head. Where the kings oppressed others the servant, possibly Israel, but in any case the bearer of Israel's destiny, is 'oppressed and afflicted' (Isa. 53.7). Where the kings received honour he is 'despised and rejected' (53.3). Where they lived by transgression he is 'wounded for our transgressions, bruised for our iniquities' (53.5). They make use of a corrupt law (Isa. 10.1) but he is 'numbered with the transgressors' (53.12). In predicating all this of the servant of YHWH, the instrument of God's purpose in human history, the same is predicated of God. God is the Lord; but he is the Lord who takes the form of the Servant. In the same way the patriarchal images of father and husband are transformed in terms of tenderness (Hos. 11. 1f.) and faithfulness (Hos. 2.19-20). Hosea refuses the apellation 'Baal', meaning 'lord' or master: 'in that day, says the Lord, you will call me, "My husband" (Ish) and no longer will you call me, "My Baal"' (Hos. 2.16).

There are, therefore, different accounts of what it means to be 'Lord' in the scriptures which Jesus and the authors of the New Testament read. There was a choice between, roughly, a Solomonic or Maccabean idea of lordship, and the reinterpretation which emerged in Second Isaiah. There is no doubt whatever as to the choice Jesus made, whether or not Isaiah 53 was an important text for him. He speaks constantly of the kingdom, but says that the rich and powerful cannot enter it (Mark 10.13,23). He promises God's blessing to the meek and powerless (Matt. 5.5,10). He extends his invitation to the least and the outcastes (Mark 2.16;Luke 14.12f.). He preaches love of the enemy and warns that anger is a form of murder (Matt. 5.21f.,38f.). He enters the Temple fulfilling the prophecy of Zechariah that Zion's king comes 'meek and riding upon an ass' (Matt. 21.4). Finally he takes up the Isaianic theme of service. 'Whoever would be great among you', he tells his followers, 'must be your servant and whoever would be first among you must be slave of all. For the Son of Man came not to be served but to serve, and to give his life as a ransom for many' (Mark 10.42f.). In Luke's variant of this story Jesus tells the disciples, 'I am amongst you as one who serves' (Luke 22.27). John gives narrative expression to this saying in the story of the foot washing (John 13.1f.).

The redefinition of power effected by Jesus was central to Paul's gospel. When he told the Christians in Philippi to 'have the mind of Christ' in them he talked about Christ 'taking the form of a slave' (Phil. 2.5-7). Because he had this mind himself he was prepared to glory in his own weakness (II Cor. 11.30f.) and saw, like Second Isaiah, a complete inversion in the notions of earthly wisdom and power:

For Jews demand signs and Greeks seek wisdom, but we preach Christ crucified, a stumbling block to Jews and folly to Gentiles, but to those who are called, both Jews and Greeks, Christ the power of God and the wisdom of God. For the

foolishness of God is wiser than men, and the weakness of God
is stronger than men (I Cor. 1.11-25).

All theologians who have written on providence are clear that
they are reflecting on God's power and wisdom. This makes it all
the more astonishing that no theologian in the classical tradition,
up to and including Barth, has attempted an exposition of
providence in terms of these verses. Covertly, appeal has always
been to the other tradition of God's power, resting on a direct and
non-inverted analogy with earthly rulers. This makes the well-
known passage from Bonhoeffer's letters, where a number of
recent accounts of providence have chosen to end, all the more
important. Though it is familiar it can bear repeating. In his
correspondence with Bethge, Bonhoeffer tried to explore what he
took to be a movement towards human autonomy in the
contemporary world, in which we have to live *etsi Deus non
daretur*:

> God would have us know that we must live as men who
> manage our lives without him. The God who is with us is the
> God who forsakes us (Mark 15.34). The God who lets us live
> in the world without the working hypothesis of God is the God
> before whom we stand continually. Before God and with God
> we live without God. *God lets himself be pushed out of the
> world, and that is precisely the way, the only way, in which he
> is with us and helps us.* Matt. 8.17 makes it quite clear that
> Christ helps us, not by virtue of his omnipotence, but by virtue
> of his weakness and suffering.
>   Here is the decisive difference between Christianity and all
> religions. Man's religiosity makes him look in his distress to
> the power of God in the world: God is the *deus ex machina*.
> The Bible directs man to God's powerlessness and suffering;
> only the suffering God can help. To that extent we may say
> that the development towards the world's coming of age
> outlined above, which *has done away with a false conception
> of God, opens up a way of seeing the God of the Bible, who
> wins power and space in the world by his weakness.*[19]

This passage has been the subject of intense discussion in the past
forty years. After some enthusiasm for the idea of a 'world come

of age' the notion has now, rightly, fallen into disfavour. Bonhoeffer's suggestions about the suffering God on the other hand are appealed to time and again, though there have been voices advising that they must be read in their context, life under the Nazis and in a prison cell, and that they do not have universal validity. Might it not be, however, that life in a prison cell is just the context which enabled Bonhoeffer to discern the essential drift of scripture, and to break with the assumptions of the metaphysical tradition? And are not the notions of the omniscience and omnicausality of God shown to be mistaken both by the devious and unconvincing logical and theological gymnastics to which they lead in order to maintain a real concept of human free will and by an exegesis of scripture which begins from the cross? It is here that any Christian doctrine of providence has to begin and not from axioms about what the knowledge and power of an infinite being 'must' be like. As Barth said about objections to the incarnation: 'We may believe that God can and must only be absolute in contrast to all that is relative, exalted in contrast to all that is lowly, active in contrast to all suffering, inviolable in contrast to all temptation, transcendent in contrast to all immanence . . . but such beliefs are shown to be quite untenable and corrupt, and pagan, by the fact that God does in fact do and be this in Jesus Christ . . . our ideas of his nature must be guided by this, and not *vice versa*.'[20] It is a pity he did not follow this advice in working out his account of providence.

The task of a Christian doctrine of providence is, then, to discern the shape of God's guidance and sustaining of all things in a way which is compatible with the cross. This sets us three related tasks: first, we need to show that the idea of a suffering God is coherent – that it would not be, as the Fathers imagined it, a contradiction in terms. Secondly, to try and see *in what sense weakness can be understood as power* both in the evolution of the universe, in human history and in our own lives. To put it another way inquiry about providence is a question of understanding what we mean when we talk of *the power of love*. Clearly, beginning from the cross does not mean replacing the 'Almighty Tyrant' with the 'Powerless Wimp'. Finally, we need an account of human freedom which is not, as Barth characterizes it, the negation of grace.

The weakness of God

Does it make sense to talk of a suffering *God*? Herbert McCabe feels that much contemporary talk on the subject is incoherent.[21] He rests his case on an appeal to what he regards as a proper agnosticism about God's nature. The word 'God' is the answer to questions like, 'Why anything rather than nothing?' or 'What does it *all* mean?'. We know that there is an answer, though we do not know what the answer is. The answer is the conclusion to all of Aquinas' so-called 'proofs' of God's existence – *et hoc omnes dicunt Deum: this everyone calls 'God'*. Whilst we must be agnostic about the nature of God we can point to things God cannot possibly be, and these include perishability, decline, dependence, and therefore suffering. We can be redeemed from misery and oppression only by the God who is *not* one of the participants in history. To lose sight of what he calls somewhat tendentiously the 'Jewish creation question' is to regress to the worship of idols. The true God can be 'in no way passive with respect to the world'. God then does not suffer, but because he holds all things in being he is 'closer to the sufferer than she is to herself'. McCabe feels that it makes perfect sense *both* to say that God does not suffer *and* to say that God has the most intimate possible involvement with the sufferings of his creatures.

Paul Fiddes, by contrast, wishes to defend not merely the possibility but the *necessity* of talk about the suffering of God, on four grounds.[22] He appeals first to what we have called the logic of love. To love is to be vulnerable, and a Being who could not be hurt could not love. Here he has the support of 'Jewish prophetic theology'. Whatever we make of it, it is clear that the prophets of Israel represent God as grievously hurt by his people, a hurt which anticipates the rejection of Jesus and Jesus' own lament over Jerusalem. The central place of the cross in Christian theology is the second reason for talk of God's suffering, a proposition with which McCabe agrees. Thirdly, he instances the demands of theodicy: the facts of human suffering constitute a sort of moral demand that God suffers alongside us. Only a God who knows suffering seems adequate to a faith which knows about Auschwitz and Hiroshima. Lastly, and more dubiously, he appeals to the history of evolution and the interiority of God to this process. Because we now think of the world as a community of relationships, we realize that the process 'requires as much sacrifice and pain as the building of any human community'.[23] But if there are good reasons to talk of God suffering does this leave us with *God*, the Creator and Sustainer of all things, rather than a very important member of the universe? Defending the proposition that God can suffer and remain God, Fiddes appeals felicitously to the 'freedom of God to be in need', and to the 'perfect incompleteness' of God. McCabe's assertion that God is in no way passive with respect to creation is presumably a way of talking of God's radical freedom. But God's freedom is his freedom to be himself and, as we see, this includes his freedom to be for us. 'It has then as little meaning to say that "he need not have loved us" as it has to say "he need not have been himself".'[24] God has freely chosen to be in need, and this includes vulnerability and the possibility of change. If God is the answer to the question 'What does it *all* mean?' then, says McCabe, whatever we mean by 'God' cannot be whatever it is that makes us ask the question in the first place. This is the ground for the exclusion of talk about suffering in God. But the God revealed in Jesus is, as Barth puts it, not a prisoner of his omnipotence. Rather, his omnipotence can be exercised in choosing need. If we understand this, Fiddes wants to argue, then we can think of creation not only as the product of God's free will, but of his will as an expression of his desire. As well as a logic of love, or perhaps as part of it, there is a logic of desire, not only of the vulnerability of love but of the need of love to share itself. Does this freedom to be in need, to be hurt, and to change at least in the sense of responding to the initiative of the creature imply an imperfection in God? Only if we work with fixed ideas of what perfection must involve. If it is the perfection of *love* with which we are concerned, however, and if there is any real analogy between divine and human love the vulnerability and need are part of perfection.

Nevertheless Plato is right that a being who could be overcome or corrupted by need, change and suffering could not help us. How then can we conceive God's transcendence over suffering in a way which still allows its reality? Two different questions are involved here. One is whether God's purposes in creation might be defeated: to this question we return in the final chapter. The other question follows from asking how it is that that suffering defeats us. The answer seems to be either that it may 'break our spirit' or that it may corrupt us, perhaps by hatred or through teaching us a love of suffering for its own sake. God would cease to be God if, as it were, his spirit was broken or his love corrupted. But it must be part of what it is to be God that this could not happen. God triumphs over suffering through the certainty of final victory. To this it could be objected that we are trying to have our cake and eat it, that we cannot at the same time talk of God's openness to change and vulnerability and yet not concede the possibility of the inner corruption which would be God's most final defeat. The answer to this can only be the appeal of faith to the fact that in Jesus it is love which is revealed as the very heart of reality. To say that God is God is to stake one's life on the impossibility of love being finally defeated precisely because it bears, believes and hopes all things. Belief in God is belief in unconquerable love, love which cannot be pushed beyond forgiveness into hatred or indifference. That than which a greater cannot be conceived is ultimate love, or love which is ultimate because it cannot surrender to negativity. 'And that we call God.'

The second way in which God overcomes suffering, according to Fiddes, is through choosing it himself. One who chooses suffering is not thereby ruled by it. This argument appeals especially to stories of torture where the acceptance of suffering by the victim robs the person who inflicts it of all of his power. Analogously it is out of his desire for his creatures that God chooses to suffer, and it is this choice which negates the destructive power of suffering.

Is the God whose omnipotence is realized in weakness also omniscient? Can we escape the logical tangle of knowledge, will and causality which led classical doctrines of providence to affirm that God predestines all things? The notion of God's omniscience flows from the same set of Platonic assumptions of the divine as the negation of all that is mutable and thinks of eternity as the 'total, simultaneous and complete possession of unlimited life' in Boethius' famous definition. This definition is unacceptable, said Barth, because it would negate the significance of the history in which God himself is involved. If God was pure eternity he would have time for us 'only apparently and figuratively'. The implication is that temporal events cannot be known and redeemed timelessly. Fiddes illustrates this point cogently in terms of a

refugee in need on Monday and relieved on Wednesday: 'If God is
to know the suffering of the man on Monday as it really is, he
cannot at the same time and in the same manner be aware of his
experience of relief on Wednesday.'[25] God's eternity is not the
negation of time but its perfection: 'As the eternal One who as
such has and himself is absolutely real time, He gives us the
relatively but in this way genuinely real time proper to us.'[26]
Barth nevertheless maintained that in God all things are *simul*.
Beginning from this teaching of God's possession of time in a
preeminent sense Moltmann has wanted to speak of 'the history
of the Trinitarian God'. God is not above the fray of universal
history but truly accompanies it. The Trinitarian life which is
revealed to us on the cross is open to our experience; it draws
human experience into itself. Moltmann has taken up themes
from the Jewish kabbalah and spoken of God finding perfection
and glory through the experience of history.[27] The necessity of
some such idea seems to be implied if there are contingent states
which are not, as it were, simply arranged to look as if they were
contingent. If God has endowed us with freedom then the pattern
of the future is worked out between God and the creature. This
does not threaten belief in God's perfection because he is perfect
as 'the origin of ever new possibilities for his world', precisely as
the one who does not need to have every detail worked out in
advance, but who can freely and sovereignly allow for surprise,
openness, novelty and chance. What makes God God is not
prediction but promise, God's *hesed* or covenant faithfulness. 'I
cannot give you up Ephraim', says YHWH to a recalcitrant
Israel, 'for I am God and not man, the Holy One in the midst of
you' (Hos. 11.8-9). The creature is creature because its hopes fail,
it gives up on those it once loved, because it does not believe in the
future. Whatever we mean by 'God' is the one who cannot and
does not do any of these things, and whose victory is in
triumphant faithfulness.

The power of God

We may accept then that to conceive of a God who suffers is not
necessarily to make God a member of this universe, as McCabe
fears. But how are we to understand God's weakness as actually
powerful not simply as a piece of rhetoric but in universal and

historical process? In the first place God's power in weakness is known in the *power of the Word*, a very particular illustration of the fact that 'the pen is mightier than the sword'.

The theme of the power of God's Word is very prominent in the Old Testament. Whilst we read about 'empty words' or 'idle words' (Isa. 36.5; Prov. 14.23) the word of God is the opposite of these: it is a true word, which is God's self expression and which has a concrete effect. It 'goes out', 'comes true', 'comes to pass', 'endures', 'runs swiftly'. The climax of the prophetic 'theology of the Word' is in Isaiah 55:

> For as the rain and the snow come down from heaven,
> and return not thither but water the earth,
> making it bring forth and sprout,
> giving seed to the sower and bread to the eater,
> so shall my word be that goes forth from my mouth;
> it shall not return to me empty,
> but it shall accomplish that which I purpose,
> and prosper in the thing for which I sent it (Isa. 55. 10-11).

God's Word effects his *purpose* (here *chapets* – what God delights or takes pleasure in). His purpose cannot be deflected (Isa. 14.24f.). How are we to understand the power of this Word in our history? We begin with the way in which this story subverts and transfigures all images of human power. This process begins in scripture itself. The image of God as the leader of a successful revolutionary war, which is essentially what we have in the Exodus stories, or the image of God as the Mighty King, are both completely transformed by identifying *victory* with the *cross*. Exactly the same goes for the power of wisdom. There is a dialectic in human history, a subtle process of exchange, between nature and nurture, the determinations of modes of production and the stories which capture human dreams for something different. This story constitutes a permanent challenge to our ideas of power and to the idols we project upon them. It keeps before our face the 'absolute future' of God's kingdom where the first come last and the last first and challenges every possible complacency. The power of the story can be seen in the way it has in fact generated revolt and protest against inhuman conditions from the time of the Israelite monarchy onwards. There a tyrannical monarchy was critiqued in the name of the God of the exodus; the group which wrote Deuteronomy could therefore insist that any king was only 'one from amongst his brethren', and could propose strict limits on royal power (Deut. 17). Similar revolts and proposals can be found in the church Fathers, in many of the mediaeval and Reformation peasant movements, in the Levellers and Diggers, and today in liberation theology. The degree to which this story constitutes a *cor inquietum* wherever it is found cannot be underestimated.

Another aspect of the power of this story is that it both tells of and thereby mediates *the power of vicarious forgiving love* which 'changes human wills and shatters proud self-enclosed egos'. This love is powerful because it turns the flank of evil. Thus in the Joseph story the climax is both that life is preserved and that the brothers are forgiven. Fiddes wants to argue that the story telling mediates or makes possible the 'exchange of feelings' involved in any true act of forgiveness. The biblical story, and particularly the gospels, tells of the exchange between God and the creature in which we are forgiven, and this generates both the inner change (conversion) which comes from knowledge of this forgiveness, and makes forgiveness possible in community. It is 'an event of such power that it is appropriate to use metaphors of victory over hostile forces to describe it'.[28] Once again we could appeal to a myriad of stories to illustrate this particular kind of power: Francis in San Damiano, Bartolomeo de las Casas in Cuba, Wesley in Oxford and even, dare one say, the young Gandhi, discovering the story of Jesus through Ruskin and Tolstoy, and from there discovering the Bhagavad Gita and a new way of reading it.

But if we grant the power of the Word, still this is clearly not enough. We have to go beyond it to the *power of a community* which does not depend on the usual trappings of power. The power of this community lies in openness and service, it lies in its very weakness. This was the power which Tertullian appealed to and Celsus recognized, despised and feared. It was the power of all the monastic movements and all the radical reform movements of the sixteenth century onwards. From this perspective we can see what a disastrous misunderstanding was implied in the high papal theology and the idea of the 'prince bishop', or in the later concordat between church and state. Those who took this road sold their birthright for a mess of pottage, abandoned the power of a community of slaves, as Jesus described them, for the illusions of a power which everyone understood only too well. Nevertheless, the community which gathers round the story is perpetually renewed and many contemporary 'root groups' and 'base communities' are rediscovering what evangelical power really amounts to.

The power of the community of which we speak is not simply the power of the church but what Gutiérrez has called '*the power of the poor in history*'.[29] Trying to understand this takes us to the heart of the gospel paradox: after all, the poor are victims, are and have been defeated day by day, 'stoned, sawn in two, killed with the sword, destitute, afflicted, ill treated' as Hebrews puts it. How can these be the victors? Gutiérrez refers to the power of their 'subversive gladness', the subversive gladness of the Magnificat or the Beatitudes. 'Blessed are you poor', says Jesus, 'for yours is the kingdom of God. Blessed are you that hunger now . . . Blessed are you that weep now' (Luke 6.20f.). Why? What is this blessedness, which is the power of the poor? Gutiérrez speaks of a fertile, creative spiritual reality which surges up from the struggles of the poor. To be sure there is a poverty and oppression, a continuation of suffering, which can be desperately dehumanizing, which can break the spirit of a people. Yet somehow 'radical hope' remains in songs and popular myths and liturgies: it is the joy of a life not corrupted by self interest, by the 'deceits of the world, the flesh, and the devil', which Jesus blesses in the beatitudes. The power of the poor is in pointing to the transcendence of life for others, the reality of a life not dominated by egotism, the supremacy of the human values of love, compassion and forgiveness over material values. Their power is in their silent witness to the way in which all power over others corrupts. The power of the poor is, then, in laying bare the very roots of what it is to be human, like removing layers of varnish from an old masterpiece, so that we can see it in all its glory. This power is not the prerogative of the Christian poor – of which there is no hint in Jesus' teaching, but of the poor as such. What the gospel reveals is that God is to be encountered in and alongside the poor, in what we find with them, in their subversive joy. Historically and universally, grace is encountered here. It is here, and on this level, that 'God is working his purpose out', that his providence may be discerned and that weakness is known as strength.

Drawing on process thought Paul Fiddes has attempted to

understand the power of weakness as the *power of persuasion* appealing to the metaphor of a 'field of force'. The life and death of Jesus constitute such a field of force which the church preserves and amplifies. This 'field of force' (again, the community) moves us to respond to God, enables us to trust him in a new way so that our perception of death is changed and we ourselves are changed.

This account of the power of persuasion clearly amounts largely to a re-statement of the 'subjective' theory of the atonement. There is nothing necessarily wrong with this. The weakness of subjectivist theories was not, as is usually said, that they were soft on sin, but that they were not always stated in terms of a theology of the Holy Spirit. The background of Abelard's notorious theology is a strong Augustinian theology of grace which understands God working ceaselessly 'from the inside' to change people. The problem with this theology is that it impales us on a dilemma: either we are led to think of God working through silent inner promptings which we cannot identify historically, and therefore to give priority to some (unspecifiable) religious experience; or we take the route of Aquinas and identify the church and sacraments as channels of grace, in which case we are but a short step from asserting that 'outside the church there is no salvation'. In the first case it is difficult to know in what the 'weakness' of God would consist for God seems to be the ultimate Hidden Persuader, and grace a form of subliminal advertising; in the second case we understand the weakness very well but it is difficult to give an account of God's work in areas and periods not touched by the gospel, not to mention the universe at large. In responding to this dilemma we have no option but to think of God at work in the whole of universal process and the whole of human history. God's real presence in the history of Israel, in Jesus, and in the sacraments cannot mean his real absence elsewhere. We can then, finally, think of *the power of God's patience*. God's *power* is seen in the fact that God does not need to resort to coercion, does not need to take short cuts. The refusal of the twelve legions of angels (Matt. 26.53) is not weakness but supreme strength. The immense length of time that God is prepared to allow for the evolution of the universe argues the unweariedness of the divine patience, as a sign and a source of omnipotence. In relation to the universe God can trust the power of 'persuasion' and does not need to 'interfere' to realize his purposes.

God the Creator is not weak, but powerful: 'all' powerful in that he has the power to realize his purposes in creation and history. Yet this power bears no resemblance to what we understand as power, the power of the mighty who are to be put down from their thrones. It is a sixfold power which triumphs through 'weakness': the power of the Word, the power of a community of the poor and of transvalued values, the power of forgiveness, the power of persuasion, and the power of the divine patience. The web of this power holds creation in being and its exercise is God's providential rule. We turn now to explore analogies by which to try and grasp this.

(handwritten margin note: No but is the struggle against life threatening poverty = the struggle of / for the poor?)

5

Divine Direction

When Barth turned to the 'How' of God's providential rule he set himself, or any possible doctrine of providence, strict limits. A properly Christian doctrine must not describe the relation between God and the creature either in terms of the relation between creature and creature, or in mechanistic terms. It must not compromise the character of the meeting between God and the creature as a genuine encounter. It must avoid the idea of divine emanations. It must speak of the divine mystery, but avoid a mere 'ignoramus'. Finally, it will be a statement of faith and involve a 'nevertheless' in the face of much hostile evidence.[1] To these conditions we must add the following: any Christian doctrine of providence must be founded on an understanding of power, and therefore of operation, which stems from the cross. At the same time it must not make God merely passive – it cannot end in Deism for 'Providence consists in action'. It must not be manipulative, leading, despite strenuous assertions to the contrary, to the view of God as the Almighty Tyrant. It must make a place for the chance which is clearly an element of world process, and for the proper autonomy of the creature. Finally, it must make sense of Christian experience, which is that all things can be brought to God in prayer. With these guidelines in mind we can turn to the analogies through which Christian tradition has sought to understand God's providence.

The use of analogies

Whoever and whatever God is, he is not a member of any universe. This sets a fundamental problem for theological language which has been classically answered by the theory of analogy. Analogy, Aquinas wants to say, is a perfectly normal feature of our language. Take a word like 'healthy' (he uses Aristotle's example here). There is a primary sense (applied to persons and animals) and a derivative sense (applied to a diet or a seaside resort) which is neither univocal nor equivocal. This intermediate sense is analogical. When we talk of a healthy diet we speak 'analogically'.[2] This gives us a clue as to how to talk about God. We take as an axiom that an effect derives from a cause and we trace a perfection back from a lower to a higher order of being (*via remotionis*). In following this procedure to talk of God we systematically eliminate imperfections in the lower order (*via eminentiae*). Thus in speaking of God as 'father' we do not attribute to him patriarchal power, impatience, selfishness or any of the other imperfections of human fatherhood. The analogy rather functions, as Patrick Sherry puts it, to 'point in the direction in which God is to be found rather than to represent him'.[3]

Fundamental as it is in everyday as well as theological speech the use of analogy has always been suspect. If the two terms of the analogy are 'partly like' and 'partly unlike' how do we know what the 'partly' means and what determines the likeness? Addressing the *analogia entis* Sherry believes that we must think in terms of sharing of some, though not necessarily all, truth conditions so that, for instance, a wise man and a wise cat would both pursue long term goals, avoid foolish actions and learn from experience. The example is felicitous because it points at once to the need to take revelation into account, as the 'wisdom' of the cross appears from most perspectives an extraordinarily foolish action. For this reason Barth preferred to talk of an *analogia fidei* in which human language suffered a 'divine takeover' in revelation so that we learn the true meaning of what it is to be wise from the biblical narrative rather than from human experience. Analogies used for God are not simply an example of projection, arising from the human need to stretch language to speak of a being who is not a member of the universe, but rather represent

God's teaching us the true way of looking at things. The analogy of faith involves the transformation of our concepts. It is *given* us; it is grace. This emendment of the classical teaching is indispensable and yet it is not the last word. That God's revelation makes analogous talk of God possible does not mean that we are restricted to the analogies we have in scripture – this would imply both a docetic view of scripture and that God did not remain continually engaged with human history. Rather, the knowledge we have of God in revelation constitutes both a springboard for further reflection and at the same time gives us the criteria with which to test this reflection. The task of seeking helpful analogies which 'point' beyond themselves to God is a permanent one.

The use of analogy is bound up with other linguistic and theoretical devices, like metaphors and models, which have this same function. A metaphor, says Janet Soskice, is a figure of speech through which we speak about one thing in terms seen to be suggestive of another.[4] They are a heuristic device bridging the gap between the known and the unknown. Models, metaphors and analogies are not the same but they are related. Thus 'fatherhood' functions as a model when used as a frame to think about God, but talk of God's loving care for his children is metaphorical. Building theories in science is a matter of constructing a proper analogy and this analogy is provided by a model.[5] Models generate webs of metaphor which are used, by the natural sciences for example, to speak of transcendent but putatively real entities or relations. Whereas for the positivist model generated questions are improper and unanswerable, and for the idealist they have no referential import, for the realist they constitute the stuff of scientific investigation, representing to thought the possible if necessarily unobservable structures of the world.[6] When we ask how metaphors can be reality depicting we need to realise that there is a separation of referring and defining at the heart of metaphorical discourse so that we can refer in the absence of an unrevisable definition. In the same way we cannot describe God but we can point to him through and beyond his effects. This is the 'use' of analogies, using the word here tendentiously to cover models and metaphors. In order to pray we need to know who God is and what he is up to. This is given us in revelation, but not in such a way that God's mystery and hiddenness is infringed. Beginning from revelation we look for models which help us to understand God's action in the world, and therefore to pray more truly. Good models, in theology as in science, 'suggest possibilities'. In scientific practice, Soskice argues, models and theory go together. 'The model or analogue forms the living part of the theory, the cutting edge of its projective capacity and, hence, is indispensable for explanatory and predictive purposes.'[7]

It is such a model that we hope to propose in an attempt to understand providence. In the tradition analogies used to speak of providence functioning in two different, though related, ways. One set tries to characterize the *nature* of God's activity, the other to illuminate the question of *how* God works. We shall take them in turn.

Analogies of rule and planning

The most common of the first type of analogy used to describe the nature of providence is political: it speaks in terms of rule or world government. Aquinas gives us a classical example. Arguing that law derives from the moral sense of the ruler of the community he goes on:

> It is clear, however, supposing the world to be governed by divine Providence . . . that the whole community of the universe is governed by divine reason. Thus the rational guidance of created things on the part of God, as the Prince of the universe, has the quality of law.[8]

According to Barth's account of the analogy of faith we look for a transformation of our concepts in an analogy which is *given* us, and a certain degree of this kind of transformation can be seen in Aquinas' use of the analogy of rule. Rule is essentially 'rational guidance of created things' rather than the exercise of power. Yet, in the first instance, much cruder ideas of rule continued to inform Christian prayer: 'O Lord our heavenly Father, high and mighty, King of kings, Lord of lords, the only ruler of princes', began the prayer for the monarch in the *Book of Common Prayer*. To be sure the eternal Sovereign is also called 'Father', and, like all analogies for God, its use in this way relativizes the power of earthly kings and princes: it is *God* who is the ultimate Lord and not them, a point of which seventeenth-century radicals were well aware. Nonetheless, this imagery automatically calls to mind the kings and lords with whom people were familiar, as mediaeval iconography demonstrates, and the kind of conclusions it legitimated can be seen in the contest between Emperor and Pope for temporal power. More significantly, the appeal to 'rational guidance' remains a very far cry from the devastating transfiguration of sovereignty which is implied by 'rule from a cross'. God's rule, if that is a proper way of speaking of God's relation to his creation, cannot be less than rational, but that rationality *is* the foolishness of God. Perhaps after all the analogy of rule, so self-evident to monarchical societies, and therefore so strongly grounded in the Old Testament and even in the New, is not in fact an appropriate way to speak of a God who 'rules' from the cross. The difficulties involved in the analogy are illustrated by the way in which Barth is seduced by it to insist that God 'decides' and 'arranges' all things and that his will is done in all things 'completely, unconditionally and irresistibly'. When he turned to the doctrine of reconciliation a year or so after completing this account of providence he found it necessary to emphasize both the paradoxical nature of God's power known in the cross and the way in which grace exalts human beings to partnership. God's omnipotence, he wrote, 'can assume the form of weakness and impotence and do so as omnipotence, triumphing in this form'.[9] Similarly when, in the next volume, he speaks of 'the exaltation of the Son of Man' he talks of God not only as the Lord but as the partner of human beings and emphasizes that grace exalts human beings to be God's fellow workers. It seems to have been assumptions about the exercise of omnipotent rule which prevented this perception in his account of providence.

Related to this analogy is the *pastoral* one so familiar to us from Psalm 23. Ezekiel in particular had spoken of the rulers of Israel as shepherds and the people as sheep, a theme taken up for reflection in John's gospel. God himself is described as the 'Shepherd of Israel' who 'leads Joseph like a flock'. And the psalmist at once goes on: 'Stir up thy might and come to save us!' (Ps. 80.1-2). The problem with the analogy is that the 'sheep' appear as completely passive. It does not seem to be the case that all we are required to do by the divine guiding is to say 'baa' and feed in green pastures. More to the point is holding on to God in the valley of the shadow.

A very profound part of being human is to make plans for the future: we cannot live purely for the present but only, rationally, with some kind of future orientation. The suggestion that God is a Planner, and providence is the working out of his plan, follows from this experience. The problem with the analogy is that whereas human plans frequently fail, it is assumed that divine plans do not, and this leads to a kind of fatalism. The word 'plan' scarcely occurs in scripture. The word translated 'plan' in Peter's speech at Pentecost (Acts 2.23) is in fact *boule*, counsel, and this suggests that we might be better to speak of a divine *purpose* rather than a plan. This would be consistent with the theme of prophetic exhortation which was, namely, that God might change his mind (e.g. Amos 5.14-15).

Langford has recently proposed a leadership analogy which in some degree incorporates aspects of all of these. Providence, he suggests, can be thought of like a climbing expedition. There is the advanced planning (God's creative and sustaining activity); there is the predictable running of the enterprise (God's action as final cause and general providence); and there are ad hoc decisions (special providence and the miraculous).[10] This analogy avoids the worst features of rule or shepherding, the tendency to absolutism on the part of God on the one hand and complete passivity on the part of human subjects on the other. Planning is included but reconciled with contingency. Its two main drawbacks are first that it is by definition 'up front' in a way which seems not to correspond with the hiddenness of God's working, what R.S.Thomas depicts as God's refusal to cheat,[11] and secondly that it lays insufficient stress on creativity. To meet both of these conditions we turn to the analogy of attraction.

The analogy of attraction

The attempt to understand God's agency in terms of attraction is an ancient one, found in different ways in both Plato and Aristotle. The problem with it is that it often depicts, in Aristotle's phrase, an *Unmoved* Mover, attracting simply as the object which inspires eros. To avoid this difficulty consider the following picture. Imagine a person walking down a street, and hearing the music of a dance from a nearby hall. Attracted by the music they walk over to see what is going on and slip inside to join the dance. This analogy emphasizes both the personal action of God in attraction, the response of the creature, and at the same time invites reflection on the modes of God's attraction.

The analogy appeals above all to John 12.32 – the crucified Christ drawing all people to himself – and to the Old Testament texts which lie behind that, such as Isaiah 60.2-3 – the nations streaming to the glory which possesses Zion. Jesus himself seems to think of the power of attraction in speaking of the disciples as a city set on a hill, or a lamp on a lampstand which cannot be hid. There is also the extremely suggestive image of Hosea, who speaks of God 'alluring' Israel, bringing Israel to the desert so that he might 'speak tenderly to her' (Hos. 2.14-15). We might also think of the use church tradition has made of the Song of Songs, where Christ addresses the church as a lover: 'Arise, my love, my fair one, and come away . . . ' (Song of Songs 2.10f.).

In a pregnant sentence Barth spoke of God's triunity as 'the secret of his beauty',[12] and this alerts us to the fact that any attempt to speak of God working through attraction has to appeal to the doctrine of the Trinity. In what sense is God's triunity a measure of his beauty? We have to look in two related directions: at the surprisingness of God, and at God's being in relation.

What Coventry Patmore ironically called the 'dry doctrine' of the Trinity is revealed in three sets of experiences which breach the status quo.[13] First, God is the one who liberates Israel from the archetypal land of standing order, Egypt, where everything is sacrally guaranteed. In such a society the past guarantees the future but YHWH 'challenges the past and everything guaranteed by it from a future which is freedom'. God is known, then, in bringing Israel from bondage into freedom.

But there is one situation where the status quo is absolute, where nothing ever changes, and that is death. The doctrine of the Trinity affirms that God is known, a second time, in raising Jesus from the dead, from that situation where the last word is spoken and the books are closed. The resurrection opens these books, denies any such last word. This is expressed beautifully by the mediaeval Latin term for what English calls 'the Last Judgment': 'novissima' – the ultimately new things (a sense preserved by Luther who spoke of 'der Jungste Tag'). As the one who raises Jesus from the dead God is known as the One who is absolutely surprising, never boring, but the source of inexhaustible life, in every sense.

Finally, God is known as Spirit sending the community beyond the boundaries of Israel with the task of breaking down all barriers and alienations, whether cultural, sexual or economic (Gal. 3.28). God is known in reconciliation, in the community which manifests the fruits of the Spirit as Paul enumerates them – love, joy, peace, patience, kindness, goodness, faithfulness, gentleness, self-control. These things spring from the 'grace' of God, his self-giving to the uttermost, his constancy (*hesed*), his mercy, his forgiveness, or as Paul also described these things, his 'righteousness'.

The beauty of God as it is disclosed in his Trinitarian revelation is then as the one who 'dissarays us with surprise', and as the one who liberates from all situations which dehumanize and bring death.

In the second place the beauty of God is his being as the one who is relationship in himself, and not as the alone with the alone. God is beautiful because God is love, and love is essentially relationship. This is the meaning of John's language about mutual indwelling and glorification (John 14.12f.). God's beauty (*kabod* or *doxa*) is known in the mutual relationship of Father, Son and Spirit, a relationship which is centred on the cross. What is beautiful is the love which forgives and pours itself out for others, and it is this love which all three persons of the Trinity *are*. Sharing in this relationship the disciples find joy because in God's presence there is always 'fullness of joy' (Ps.16.11). God is the most beautiful of the objects of human contemplation because as self-giving, purpose free but purposeful love in himself he is the source of our joy. Love has this character because it is of its essence both to will and to share the good not 'for' anything but 'simply for joy'. The metaphor of light or brightness often associated with beauty, and insisted on by Aquinas, signifies the self-evidential character of beauty. Thus for John it is the self-evidential beauty of the cross which will draw all people to Christ – and it is this which is the profoundest link between the Trinity and providence.

If we follow this analogy then we can understand the autonomy of creation as a gracious gift. Autonomy does not mean, as it did in Deism, that God begins the process and then withdraws, which would not be gracious at all. Nor does it mean that God's prerogative is in some way infringed, as Barth seems to imagine. Rather, it means that God chooses to work through the billions of years of evolution or through human free will because he refuses to manipulate or control but rather wishes to woo creation to conformity with his son, as Hosea suggests.

The analogy of attraction is both immensely illuminating and indispensable. It points us to many of the levels of God's power in weakness which we explored in the last chapter, particularly to the 'power of the redemptive story'. Nevertheless, it falls short of the 'direction, control and guidance' which the *Oxford English Dictionary* correctly offers as a definition of providence. In an attempt, again, to meet these shortcomings we move to our controlling analogy which is suggested by Peter Brook's brilliant essay on theatre, *The Empty Space*.[14]

Divine direction

C. S. Lewis suggested that the analogy of the Potter and the pot might be pressed to speak of the relation of God and creation in terms of that between an artist and his or her product, an analogy which, as we have seen, is decisive for Aquinas. The seventeenth-century Divine, Sherlock likewise favoured this analogy and pointed out that it suggests that God works within chosen limitations and that these limitations may contribute to what is created.[15] If, however, we follow tradition and think of the artist using a musical instrument, or paint, wood or stone, then, like the pastoral analogy, this implies far too passive a role on the side of creation. It becomes extremely illuminating, however, when we think of arts which involve eliciting a response such as theatre direction, choreography or conducting, an analogy already suggested by Shakespeare's profound reflection on providence, theatre and divine power, *The Tempest*.

'It is a strange role, that of director', writes Peter Brook. 'He does not ask to be God and yet his role implies it.'[16] In speaking of 'God' Brook probably has in mind a being with all the answers, and yet his whole essay on theatre and direction, according to which the director succeeds only by sharing his or her *fallibility* (for which the theological correlate would be the divine 'weakness') is profoundly suggestive for doctrine of providence. Out of many possible themes I shall highlight four.

Brook's artistic career has been a sustained attack on what he calls 'deadly theatre', theatre in which there is no real event between players and audience but simply a hollow spectacle. According to him the director who comes to the first rehearsal with all the moves and business noted down (rather like Calvin's God), is 'a real deadly theatre man'. Brook describes how, on the evening of his first rehearsal with the Royal Shakespeare Company, he spent his entire time pushing little cardboard models of the actors around trying to get the shape of the first scenes in his mind. Next morning, with his prompt book in front of him, and the appropriate sequences of moves, A, B and C, he asked the actors to do what he had worked out for them: 'As the actors began to move I knew it was no good. These were not remotely like my cardboard figures, these large human beings thrusting themselves forward, some too fast with lively steps I had not foreseen, bringing them suddenly on top of me . . . We had only done the first stage of the movement, letter A on my chart, but already everyone was wrongly placed and movement B could not follow.' He felt lost and panicky, but then, 'I stopped, and walked away from my book, in amongst the actors, and I have never looked at a written plan since'.[17]

This story is a marvellous parable of God's activity. If we do in fact learn about God, and the mode of God's activity from Christ then it should be clear that God rejected the prompt book option from the very beginning, and has been from the start 'in amongst the actors'. God works without script and without plan but with, to continue the metaphor, a profound understanding of theatre and the profoundest understanding of the play. The theme of the play is love, and the realization of love. In his moving and often painful account of Brook's production David Selbourne records how Brook demanded that the actors find the 'inner impulse' of their part, of the play, and of the rhythm of their lines. Interestingly Brook remarked early on in rehearsal that there was a particular rhythm to be found and a particular actor to find it, and this demanded 'an almost metaphysical explanation'.[18] All the director can do is illuminate the play and demand that the actors find their own inner resources. Often Brook simply sat in front of the stage drumming out a rhythm. Something like this is what God demands of us. With his cardboard models Brook was actually preparing prompts for a puppet theatre – exactly the mistake so many theologians have made in their understanding of the 'theatre' of world 'history, encouraged by the classical analogies for God's activity. 'To love within the growth of a community', writes Paul Fiddes, arguing that God must be subject to change, 'is to allow it to develop in its own way and to make its own impact and contribution; otherwise it is not a community of free persons but a puppet show.'[19] Like Brook's cardboard models the possibility of a community of persons in the creator's mind cannot be quite the same as the actuality – these actors moving too fast or too slow, grouping themselves according to their own dynamics.

Against *this* analogy it might be objected that it conceives God as simply one agent amongst many, just as Selbourne sometimes wondered whether Brook was one actor amongst many. This would reduce God to the status of a finite being.[20] The giveaway here is the 'simply'. God is indeed one agent amongst many, but he is the only unique agent, just as there is only one 'director'. 'God' is the Creator and Sustainer, present in the personal reality of his graciousness to all things, and interacting with, and reacting to all things.

A second aspect of Brook's account of direction which is suggestive for theology is that it is not simply a matter of 'letting be'. When a director speaks of 'letting the play speak for itself' says Brook, suspicions are aroused, because this is the hardest job of all. 'If you just let a play speak, it may not make a sound. If what you want is for the play to be heard, then you must conjure its sound from it. This demands many deliberate actions . . .'[21] The worst director of all is the honourable unassuming one, the one who cultivates non-intervention as a way of 'respecting' the actor. The idea that a company or an actor can do without leadership he calls a 'wretched fallacy'. Just so could we describe the theological position of Deism, which believes that the autonomy of the universe is only respected by God's non-intervention. The God presented by Maurice Wiles, for instance, falls exactly into the category of the 'honourable unassuming' director. Against such a view, and pressing Brook's analogy, we believe that without divine direction there would really be 'no speech nor language'. Like the good director God must be capable of 'imposing his will', in the way in which the Joseph story, for instance, suggests. The question is, how is this done without resorting to *force majeure* or manipulation – a question both for the theatre director and for God. The answer, to draw a third lesson from Brook, is in terms of mutual exploration between director and actor:

> The director must look for where the actor is messing up his own right urges – and here he must help the actor to see and overcome his own obstacles. All this is a dialogue and a dance between director and player. A dance is an accurate metaphor, a waltz between director, player and text. Progression is circular, and deciding who's the leader depends on where you stand. The director will find that all the time new means are needed . . . He will follow the natural principle of rotation of crops: he will see that explanation, logic, improvisation, inspiration are methods that rapidly run dry and he will move from one to the other.[22]

Just so may God be conceived to work. The dialogue between director and player is prayer, which Baelz calls 'a creative participation in divine activity', but which he might also understand as divine participation in human activity. Thus Buber spoke of an 'I and Thou' between God and human beings, resulting in what he called 'active history' – an 'I' and a 'Thou' which is genuinely mutual, and through which God's purpose is fulfilled in and through human purpose. Because this is a real dialogue there must be an element of genuine surprise for God as well as for the creature. The God of Surprises also knows what it is to be surprised by joy. This in no way implies an imperfection on God's part, as the classical theology imagined. On the contrary it is precisely God's freedom in this regard which constitutes his perfection.

The question of moving from one method to another in the course of producing a play resembles what Peacocke refers to, more drily, as God's 'shuffling the pack'.[23] The art of direction is recognizing that there is a right time for everything: a time for waiting, a time for silence, a time for pushing, a time for repetition, a time for freedom, a time for discipline. Love is supremely inventive and it is God's inventiveness together with his patience which constitutes his true infinity. There is no almighty tyrant but there is a divine director, in amongst the actors, endlessly resourceful in creativity, full of humour, compassion, himself the truth which is at the heart of 'holy theatre'. Railing against the sterility of theatre before the war, says Brook (as Muir railed against the sterility of Calvinist orthodoxy) Antoine Artaud 'wrote tracts describing from his imagination and intuition another theatre – a Holy Theatre in which the blazing centre speaks through those forms closest to it. A theatre working like the plague, by intoxication, by infection, by analogy, by magic; a theatre in which the play, the event itself, stands in place of a text'.[24] Here is the rapprochement between direction and attraction. At best the two become one, as they do in all true education for 'education proceeds only by desire' as Simone Weil put it. Christian mission perhaps offers an illustration of God's providence in action for, properly understood, it works only 'by intoxication, by infection, by magic'. Mission understood as crusade is deadly theatre in every sense of the word, a crashing failure of the imagination required to get inside and alongside God's purposes as they are revealed in Christ.

Finally, Brook gives an importance to the notion of limits which the more mechanical image of God as the steersman operating between two banks of a river is unable to do. The purpose of exercises in rehearsal, he says, is to increase resistance by limiting alternatives and then to use this resistance in the struggle for true expression.[25] This suggests that the limits involved in creation may be the most positive vehicle for both divine and human creativity. Brook talks not only about holy, but about rough theatre, the theatre improvised from the back of a cart or in an upstairs room, the theatre where the audience joins in and answers back. Creation, and human history is both the holy and the rough theatre of God, for ultimately rough and holy theatre cannot be separated. There are moments, says Brook, when a performance becomes a total experience, when the divisions between deadly, rough and holy theatre become nonsense. 'At these rare moments, the theatre of joy, of catharsis, of celebration, the theatre of exploration, the theatre of shared meaning, the living theatre are one.' But then, he goes on, 'the moment is gone and it cannot be recaptured slavishly by imitation – the deadly creeps back, the search begins again.'[26] This is a parable of both the Christian life and the life of the church which is always, as Alan Ecclestone has said, a matter of having the courage to begin again. Is it not clear that the work of the Holy Spirit is a resistance to deadly theatre – again signified parabolically by what happens ever and again to the church's liturgy. But 'deadly theatre' is part and parcel of life: the routines into which relationships get trapped, the sanctification of traditions within cultures, 'time honoured norms' in law and politics, all can be forms of deadliness. Life only exists where the search begins again, and this is as true for God as for the creature. Jesus offers 'life in all its fullness', as John puts it (John 10.10), because the possibilities of exploration within the divine reality (which is love) are literally infinite. There is no end to the possibilities of exploration within God. To think of God in terms of the theatre director, then, is to think of one whose job it is to evoke talents, skills and capabilities the creature (who remains the 'actor') did not know it had. It gives God a supremely active and creative role, leading and being alongside as Orthodoxy conceived it (*praecurrit et concurrit*), but does not destroy the autonomy of the creature. It is creative without being manipulative. It insists on attraction but is not the Perfect Beauty of Plato which simply has to be to attract. If there is any validity in arguments from creation to a Creator at all then it must be clear, both from the course of evolution and from human history, that this Creator is in favour of rough, and therefore holy, theatre. But if this analogy is a pointer to the *nature* of providence *how* is this worked out?

How does God work?

'Who is this who darkens counsel by words without knowledge?' says God to Job out of the whirlwind (John 38.2). This question seems to attend any attempt to probe what is properly recognized to be the mystery of the divine working, and yet, as Barth has said, we cannot simply be content with an 'ignoramus'.

Given the caveats we have already introduced with regard to the idea of 'cause' are there analogies which help us to grasp the mode of God's working? Langford instances three which are taken from the realm of the physical sciences: the traditional comparison of God's action to that of the wind or sun, or to the force of gravity. Langford himself offers us the analogy of the tide, which both envisages a steady divine 'pressure' on events, but at the same time allows for individual variations, and even for some apparently astonishing events such as the coming of a tidal bore. As illustrations of such a 'pressure' operating in history he later offers the need to find food resources, or the human drive to know, but then, as he observes, 'the alleged working of providence is so immanent within the process that it seems hard to distinguish providence from the very laws that describe the process'.[27] All these analogies are vitiated, however, by the fact that God's action is conceived impersonally and thus easily suggest some kind of pantheism rather than the living God of biblical revelation.

Much the most important analogy is that of the relation of mind, or spirit, and body. Mind affects the material in ways that are both completely obvious and yet remain deeply mysterious. Completely materialist accounts of mind in terms, for instance, of electrical impulses in the brain, remain unconvincing: the whole remains obstinately greater than the sum of the parts. If mind cannot be explained wholly in material terms, and if it yet bears on the material, and if God is properly conceived as personal, then the obvious suggestion is that God might bear upon creation as mind bears on matter. Three disadvantages attend the analogy. In the first place we cannot think of the universe as God's body, which would be pantheism, and which would make all events in some sense expressions of God's will. Any kind of pantheism is incompatible with the view we presuppose that God is not a member of the universe, and that therefore creation is 'from nothing'. Another limitation is that since we do not know how mind works, the analogy cannot possibly function to illustrate how God works but merely to show that it is conceivable that he does. The analogy is also potentially misleading if it becomes yet another attempt to do theology by doing (in this case rather disreputable) science. It is not intended to assert that the universe is governed by telekinesis, that God is the Supreme 'Mind Bender'.

In this connection it might be helpful to make a distinction between mind and spirit. By 'spirit' here we mean something like personality: who the person has become through social conditioning as well as genetic make up. It is clear that character traits like optimism or pessimism have psychic correlates which can be affected by drugs, but it is not clear that a purely psychological account of them can be given. If 'spirit' denotes our transcendence of our genetic inheritance then we have to say that spirit clearly bears on the material, as courage and optimism can make a real difference to medical recovery. The analogy of the relation of mind or spirit to the material can then be taken further in that creation 'out of nothing' suggests an interiority of creation to the divine which makes it especially illuminating. It is not that, as process theology suggests, all 'events' (including stones) have a 'mental pole' but that, insofar as creation is the free creation of the God who is other than it, he retains a completely intimate relationship with every aspect of its being. *Because* the world is God's creation there is no 'mere' matter but everything has a living relation to him. As Aquinas puts it: 'since God is the proper cause in all things of their whole very "isness", than which nothing is more intimate or interior, it follows that he innermostly acts in all things.[28] Just as the person we are, therefore, with its social conditioning, its depressions and exhilarations, bears on the quarks and gluons which in some sense compose our body and which will 'return to dust' when we are cremated, so 'the Eternal Personal', as H. H. Farmer called God, bears on the universe which is completely his creation. It is this action which was discussed traditionally as God's use of secondary causes, the affirmation that God's purpose is achieved without manipulation but through the normal functions of the created order.

The temptation in the present century has been to follow a suggestion of Maimonides and to suppose that God relates primarily, if not only, to persons, that, as it were, for God too there is an 'I-Thou' and an 'I-It'. Are there grounds for such a belief? The suggestion can best be tested by asking how God can be conceived to relate to the processes of evolution.

Providence and evolution

In raising the question of evolution we are not asking whether the data of the history of evolution confirm or disconfirm belief in providence. The question is rather what God was doing, in the 10,000,000,000 years of evolution before the appearance of homo sapiens? We cannot be content with Augustine's facetious, 'Getting ready a hell for the inquisitive'. On the one hand it seems *prima facie* plausible to suggest that the advance of the various 'levels' of creation, from physical to chemical to biological to social in ways which are open upwards but cannot be reduced downwards, seems to move in a 'God-ward' direction so that 'we are more likely to see the mind of God at work in the unpredictability of free human beings than in the unpredictability of sub-atomic particles'.[29] In that case the immense length of time involved in evolution, which includes the massive extinctions which occurred from time to time, indicates the fact that God chooses to work through natural processes and development, to 'step back' from creation. To take up the analogy of direction it is the moment when the director sits silent, like Brook rehearsing the Dream, merely beating a rhythm on a small drum. We might say that we learn from this of God's patience and his respect for the freedom of creation. Having determined the initial conditions it may be that God waits, as it were, for the arrival of a creature with whom he can most deeply interact. Once homo sapiens comes on the scene then evolution moves to some extent from the biological sphere to the social and political – it enters the sphere of conscious choice. Then it is through influencing us that God influences the world.

Tempting as this option is the 'stepping back' obviously involves a Deism at one remove. It seems to imagine God as absent or 'resting' during the process of evolution, preceding the appearance of creatures who could pray. Whilst we have to respect scientific objections to a 'God of the gaps' – the idea for instance that the 'epistemological gap' of which evolutionary theorists speak can be filled by God's 'hidden hand' – theologically Deism will not do. Traditional discussions talked of God 'preserving and sustaining' all things, and this language rested on the perception that creation from nothing, creation by God's 'Word' – which is to say his will, joy and desire – implied the most intimate relationship of dependence between God and what was created. For God, nothing created is foreign to him. The problem is not to understand God's *relation* with the creature but the creature's *autonomy*, its God given *freedom*. How is this freedom related to God's constantly sustaining love? To say that the universe functions according to natural laws (has freedom) and yet that God exercises his providence within it (sustains it) poses primarily not a scientific but a *theological* problem. The 'God of the gaps' is a problem both because the scientist suspects that her theory will eventually embrace all reality, but also because there are no 'gaps' in God's relation to creation. The theory that God works through secondary causes is a venerable but perhaps clumsy way of meeting this difficulty, distinguishing as it does between efficient causes, which are the concern of the sciences on the one hand, and the 'final cause' of God's attractiveness on the other, which is not. Langford maintains that it is part of the very nature of providence that it operates in such a way that a naturalistic explanation of all events can be given. Providence is not another physical factor to be placed alongside gravity, wind, temperature and so on but speaks of God's use of such factors.[30] But as he admits, if God really bears on creation then 'naturalistic' cannot mean 'complete'. If a cause is an intelligibility to be grasped and if God is in some way 'in amongst the actors' in evolution as in history, then there will be a factor in the ultimate intelligibility of all things susceptible of 'eschatological' if not of present verification.

The only analogy which will help us grasp this problem is the relation of the divine and the human in Jesus of Nazareth. Jesus is not partly human and partly divine, a sort of divine-human Centaur, but one hundred per cent human and one hundred per cent divine. That this claim might be sense rather than nonsense rests, as Herbert McCabe has insisted, on an adequate doctrine of God. Such a doctrine will affirm that God is, in two of Barth's phrases, first, the 'Wholly Other', and then 'the One who loves in freedom'. Because God is the 'Wholly Other' there is not the same contradiction in claiming that Jesus is both human and divine that there would be if we claimed he was both a man and a sheep. Humans and sheep, as McCabe argues, are both members of the same universe; God is not a member of any universe. This fact is what 'Spirit' language, as opposed to psychological language, tries to articulate. It points to a different realm to our space time universe and affirms the interaction of that realm with this realm, pre-eminently in the incarnation, but analogously with all reality. Jesus was human: no natural laws were breached in his psychology or physical composition. He was also 'divine' in that the divine, the Wholly Other, shaped and fashioned his very being. The freedom of the creature Jesus of Nazareth was identical with the freedom of the Creator: this is what it means to say that he was and is 'of one substance' with the Father. By virtue of this conjunction of freedoms God's will is done perfectly in the man Jesus. Nowhere else in creation is this conjunction of freedoms perfect. We do not have to postulate 'resistance' on the part of the non-human creation to account for this. Rather, the 'levels' of creation include greater and lesser degrees of freedom, response and resistance. As the One who loves in freedom God calls into being a universe which evolves towards 'perfect freedom', first of all in the emergence of increasingly sophisticated forms of life and then in the human moral, religious, philosophical, cultural and scientific quest. The freedom of God interacts with this increasing freedom until finally this interaction can become complete at a certain stage of human development, and does so in Jesus. This is not to say that the creature 'evolves' into the divine, but that the capacity for creation to become 'God bearer' increases. What was God doing during the unimaginable span of evolution? Positing all things in his freedom he interacts with all things in their freedom. This interaction is 'spiritual', pertaining to a realm which cannot be measured by science, and certainly not by psychology, but which bears on the whole created universe, including the psyche. In human beings we see evidence of it, for instance, in true holiness, and we discern other forms in every type of creativity, in everything which creates and gives life. It is absolutely familiar and absolutely mysterious. It defies no natural laws and yet it achieves astonishing results, on the individual level, where we most commonly recognize it, but also on the historical and universal level. It is not so much a question of maintaining agnosticism about the fundamental nature of the universe but more a recognition of the *reality* of God's relationship to all things. This relationship woos, attracts or directs (in Brook's sense) all things to itself. Through it, the resistance of created freedom is overcome and God's purpose is achieved. And this is the divine providence.

6

For What Can We Pray?

The revision of the Litany of the *Book of Common Prayer* reveals a considerable hesitancy with regard to the doctrine of providence. Gone is the prayer for deliverance from lightning and tempest, plague, pestilence and famine; gone the prayer for the preservation of women in childbirth; gone the prayer that God will 'give and preserve to our use the kindly fruits of the earth'. Amongst the 'Prayers for Various Occasions' there are no prayers for rain or good weather nor do we appear to believe that it is God's gift that 'the earth is fruitful, beasts increase, and fishes do multiply'. These omissions can be accounted for partly by the advance of science, and in particular medical and agricultural science, on the one hand, and partly by a desire not to fall back on to the 'God of the gaps' on the other. Assumptions about what it is we think God can or does do clearly lie behind them, assumptions which touch the deepest nerve of Christian faith. Belief in providence, we have said, is not just the belief that God guides events and achieves his purposes through them, but that we can bring all things to him in prayer. But what are we doing when we do this? Does the doctrine of 'man come of age' mean that we must reject as childish and immature belief in a God to whom we can appeal in every situation? Should we pray only for inner strength, power to love and to forgive? Or do rationalist assumptions lie behind this practice? In failing to pray for rain do we simply parade our unbelief? Are we children of the Enlightenment too clever by half? Or is it that we have been made cynical by the terror of history amongst which we live? If I pray for trivial things, for instance to get a lift whilst hitch-hiking, or to find a lodging in a crowded city, and if I believe that success in such cases is an answer to prayer, why is it that God could not have stopped the murder of six million Jews, or the apalling accidents and tragedies which meet us day by day in the newspapers? When I pray that my children may be kept safe, what do I expect God to do?

Distilling a beautiful discussion of the prayer of Jesus by Jon Sobrino we can highlight four criteria for what he considers to be authentic Christian prayer. First, it must not be like the prayer of the Pharisee in Jesus' parable (Luke 18.11). Here prayer 'is merely a mechanism for narcissism and self-gratification. It is an exercise in self-deception . . . we can pray only insofar as we focus on someone or something other than ourselves'.[1] Secondly, Jesus' warning against empty repetition in prayer (Matt. 6.7) is understood as directed against 'the pagan idea of wearing God down under a barrage of words'.

> The positive feature in the prayer of petition is the fact that it reveals our discernment of God's will, and of God himself as someone who ever remains greater than us. It is not a matter of looking for something that we want, of an egocentric search for some satisfaction. Our Father 'knows what you need before you ask him'. In our prayer of petition we try to discover something that our Father knows already. That is what we ask him to reveal and grant. Human psychology being what it is, it is obvious that this basic petition will find expression in the concrete petitions and desires of the person who is praying. But there can be only one basic petition: 'Your will be done.'[2]

Thirdly, Sobrino cites Jesus' word that 'None of those who cry out, "Lord, Lord" will enter the kingdom of God but only the one who does the will of my Father in heaven' (Matt. 7.21). 'Mere appeals to God are useless; they must embody and go hand in hand with real life practice . . . Matthew's text stresses the ultimate importance of praxis; without it, prayer cannot express anything that is of ultimate importance.'[3] Finally, in his discussion of Gethsemane, Sobrino asserts that 'non-knowing is an essential feature of Jesus' prayer . . . it becomes part of a deeper knowledge of the Father'.[4] Jesus respects God's 'holy and unmanipulable mysteriousness'. His prayer is primarily a matter of seeking out God's will and having joy at the approach of the kingdom. It is the attempt 'to bring together the total sum of meaningfulness and the meaning of the totality'.[5] The impossible which God can do (Mark 10.27) is not, as Braun put it, 'supernatural events coming from a world beyond and producing weird consequences in this world' but that 'the poor, the impious and the wicked can unexpectedly go back to calling themselves human beings once again'.[6] God is love and what that means is discovered through the practice of love of the neighbour:

> Corresponding to a God who is truly 'greater' than human beings means responding to the demands laid down by love . . . the basic locale for his prayer was the place where the kingdom was being fashioned into reality. That place was to be found in the praxis of hearing the word of God and in the praxis of love. The God of Jesus is a greater God, with a concrete will for his kingdom. Hence Jesus' prayer is a quest for his will and submissiveness to it. That is the concrete way in which he allows himself to be overtaken by God's transcendence.[7]

Sobrino makes us face the question whether much Christian prayer of petition is not simply egotism, immaturity, escapism and ultimately superstition. Undoubtedly his emphasis on the necessary interrelationship of prayer and praxis is properly stated. Two questions attend his account in turn: first, does he do justice to Jesus' teaching on petitionary prayer? 'And he told them a parable', writes Luke, 'to the effect that they ought always to pray and not lose heart' (Luke 18.1). Is it really the case that Jesus' repeated instruction to ask, his telling of the parables of the importunate widow or the neighbour coming in the middle of the night, can be reduced to submission to God's will? True, God knows what we have need of – this is a function not of his omniscience but of his wisdom – but this does not rule out the need for prayer. On the contrary, with the Reformers and with Barth we have to understand prayer, and specifically the prayer of petition, as based on a command. 'Call upon me in the day of trouble: I will deliver you, and you will glorify me' (Ps. 50.15). Jesus' teaching on prayer rests upon many such admonitions in the tradition which shaped him. We are *commanded* to pray and in the face of the command rationalist objections fall away. The command reveals that God chooses to work with us, and not without us. Prayer is a special form of that interaction between the free and active God and the free and active creature which keeps all creation in being. As Barth puts it, it is the 'innermost centre of the covenant between God and man'.[8] When Paul speaks of the Spirit of God praying through us he is saying that prayer is *given* us as a way of sharing in the fashioning of the world. Once human beings learn to pray the future is fashioned between God and the creature together. Human asking becomes 'a movement in the cycle which goes out from God and returns to God', in other words in the outworking of providence.[9] Far from this being a Pelagian assault on God's grace it is the profoundest recognition of the creative power of the divine love. This love does not need to feel 'threatened' by human beings. Barth himself stated this impressively: God does not act in the same way whether or not we act, he wrote. 'Prayer has an influence on the action, on the very existence, of God. That is the meaning of the word "answering".'[10] 'If ever there was a miserable anthropomorphism, it is the hallucination of a divine immutability which rules out the possibility that God can let Himself be conditioned in this or that way by his creature.'[11] Doubt on God's desire to share with us in this way is the confusion of God with an immovable idol.

Secondly, does not Sobrino end up by making God too inactive? True again, God is not to be manipulated: the idea that he can be is the basic mistake of magic. But Sobrino seems to leave God's action entirely in the hands of human beings. Pushed further back this would seem to leave God absent from the billions of years of the universe's evolution as well – in which case we are back with Deism.

It is true that if we followed Sobrino's account (and like much liberation theology he echoes the liberal theology of someone like Bultmann here) there would be no problem of prayer and providence: prayer is simply a question of learning maturity in love. Providence is a problem only when we believe in a God who acts and who responds to prayer. If both our experience and our reading of revelation, which is to say the life and teaching of Jesus read in relation to the rest of scripture, compels us to believe that

God does so act and respond, what sense do we make of it? For what can we pray? In seeking an answer we follow the divisions suggested by the biblical account of God's sovereignty, asking how prayer relates to the natural order, the guiding of history, and God's providential guidance of the individual. We begin with the question of whether it makes sense to pray for rain.

Can we pray for rain?

[handwritten margin note: Austin Farrar — miracles are an enhancement of creation]

The city of Madurai is situated in south India roughly three hundred miles south of Madras, and just in the rain shadow of the Western Ghats. Rain is irregular and unpredictable, and there are frequently prolonged droughts. In these situations the local Council of Churches meets to pray for rain. Spectacular downpours of rain have occasionally been known more or less to follow this prayer. Is there an 'intelligibility to be grasped' between these two events? The temptation to appeal to a 'God of the gaps' with regard to the weather is especially great as there are still large areas of uncertainty about what actually trigger specific weather patterns, and some scientists appeal to 'chaos theory' to explain it. Nevertheless, a rough account of what happens to produce a downpour is certainly available: it relates to the rotation of the earth and the difference in temperature between the poles and the equator. If, then, we pray for rain are we asking God for some 'fine adjustment' of these universal factors to produce rain at precisely this spot and at this time? The various answers available from the tradition are not encouraging. We could say that the shower over Madurai was planned from all eternity – the solution of determinism. But then so was this famine and that earthquake with all their attendant human misery. Or we could say that the shower occurred in response to the vigil of prayer, which would be the solution of occasionalism, the doctrine that God intervenes at will here and there. This leaves us, it might be said, with both a capricious God and a capricious universe, at least insofar as other drought stricken areas did not get rain. If we limit the scope of God's intervention in some way still in the first place the autonomy of creation seems to be compromised, and secondly there is the question why he does not do so a great deal more often. Or finally we could say that the shower happened in accordance with natural laws, and that this was a lucky

[handwritten margin notes: not violation of nature but giving more of what was given. "God makes creature make itself" were participating in creative energy: were asking for an enhancement of what is already here]

coincidence. If we go on to say – 'and things only ever happen according to natural laws' – we seem to be committing ourselves to Deism.

Given the unacceptability of the first option (determinism) it is the latter two which have to be explored. The acceptance of natural law can indeed commit us to Deism. Thus in commenting on the petition, 'Give us this day our daily bread', Maurice Wiles maintains that we are simply 'acknowledging the givenness of the world'. The prayer is really a mnemonic to remind us of the importance of co-operative human labour and that a radical reordering of priorities is called for in our world.[12] Grateful as one is for this rapprochement between liberal and liberation theology, and crucial as the relation between prayer and action is, it remains a question whether acceptance of a law governed universe limits our praying in this way. Theologically, 'natural laws' need to be understood as grace. A universe which was fundamentally unpredictable would be capricious, not gracious, and would not constitute a feasible environment for the growth of a creature who could respond to God in love. But the lawful nature of the universe does not preclude the possibility that prayer may affect it.

H. H. Farmer argued that it is through his relation with mental entities that God interacts with his creation and that prayer is the nub of this relation. Prayer is 'a relation of the will of man to the will of God, and, through the will of God, to all living creativeness of nature. At its highest it is the throwing of the whole personality into the creativeness of God'.[13] Farmer takes the Exodus as an illustration of this. How could God so enter into a general meterological situation that the outcome was different from what it would otherwise have been, so falsifying the weather forecasts at Pharaoh's court? Farmer's suggestion is that God so uses his rapport with the inner reality of the natural order that their routine activities are not overridden but redirected. 'Just as man brings about effects in nature which would not otherwise happen by re-directing its routines in relation with one another, so does God, except that God acts from the inside, so to say, by inner rapport and not by external manipulation in the gross.'[14] Prayer may thus be the factor through which God directs things but, in an important phrase, Farmer talks about *hygienic limits* to prayer, defined by the divine purpose of fashioning human

personalities in love. Thus we pray for the recovery of someone
with typhoid, but not for the new growth of an arm which has
been amputated. Israel could perhaps pray for a change in the
weather at the Sea of Reeds but it makes no sense to do so where
there is no recorded rainfall. God could not grant such petitions
without denying his nature and the purpose of his providence.
But what then do we pray for?

In the tradition about Jesus we have on the one hand an
affirmation of natural law, the graciousness of the natural order:
he talks of God causing the sun to rise and rain to fall on just and
unjust (Matt. 5.45), and denies that an accident like the collapse
of a building might be a punishment for sin (Luke 13.4). Thus we
can say that drought in Bihar does not indicate that Christians
there are less fervent in prayer than elsewhere, or that the
marvellous climate of California has anything to do with the
godliness of the people there. On the other hand there is the story
of the stilling of the storm, and the disciples ask, 'Who then is this
that the wind and sea obey him?' (Mark 4.41). If it is indeed true
that the universe is interior to God as we have argued then it need
not be in the least surprising that what we understand as
'spiritual' forces (which, once again, are not identical with
psychic forces – telekinesis is not in view) are part of the dynamics
of reality. Our understanding of the universe would then be
incomplete until it took these – theological – factors into account.
It might then be that within the regularities which God has
established, which form the environment where faith, hope and
love would be possible, prayer is given us as a way in which we
can share in the direction of all things. But God asks us, as it were,
to respect the world he has given us. He does not permit himself
arbitrary miracles (cf. Matt. 26.53) and this self limitation
constitutes the proper limits of our prayer. Both in his self-
limitation and in his choosing to work together with the creature
rather than over its head we can see what the 'weakness' (which is
power) of God might mean for this aspect of providence. If,
again, we do not understand prayer as, in Baelz' phrase, putting a
coin in the slot, but more like the struggle with God of Jacob at
Bethel or Jesus in Gethsemane then, *within the limits God has set
for himself, as we understand them from both revelation and
from science*, we should pray for all sorts of things. In particular
we need to rid ourselves of the 'sophisticated adult' fallacy, which

feels that there are some things which are really too trivial to bother God with. On the contrary 'practising the presence of God' means that we habitually bring every single thing, no matter how trivial, to God – even if this only teaches us to laugh at ourselves. Barth recalls the American general who prayed for deliverance from 'this untimely rain' during the Ardennes offensive of 1944.[15] And if we are faithful to Jesus, prayer cannot be reduced simply to the petition, 'Your will be done': there is a very proper hammering at the gates of heaven. 'Your will be done' is what follows our prayer of asking. It is confidence that God will hear our prayer and answer it in his wisdom. 'We do not know how to pray as we ought', says Paul in Romans (8.26).

> Man might ask God for anything. The whole of human egoism, the whole of human anxiety, cupidity, desire and passion, or at least the whole of human short-sightedness, unreasonableness and stupidity, might flow into prayer (and that by divine commandment!), as effluent from the chemical factories of Basel is discharged into the Rhine . . . But if God is not uneasy in this regard, we certainly need not be.[16]

God orders, purifies and sanctifies our asking, in this as in all else making good what we do badly. The need to submit ourselves to this 'ordering and cleansing', to examine our requests in the light of obedience; to come not only with petition but in thanksgiving and repentance – all this stands. But it does not stand *in the way* of our asking, but if we ask in faith we learn it *through it*.

Many of these considerations also bear on the question of what we pray for for ourselves, but we are, in this next section, concerned more particularly with miracle and human freedom.

Can we pray for healing?

Bartholomew points out that infant mortality must have been very high in first-century Nazareth, and yet Jesus survived his childhood. Was this chance, or the result of providential 'protection'? If it was the latter why did God protect Jesus but not other children, who died? If on the other hand it was chance this seems to call into question the significance of the incarnation as a unique act of redemption. Bartholomew raises the question whether there might have been several 'attempts which failed', just as the

Talmudists suggested that several attempts at creation might have preceded the present one.[17] This raises once again the question of the chance which is an inescapable part of our understanding of world process. How are chance and providence compatible other than, as Arthur Peacocke puts it, God's way of 'shuffling the pack'? What is the relation of a world of chance to our prayers for healing or protection?

When Paul wrote that 'in everything God works for good with those who love him' (Rom. 8.28) he did not mean that God miraculously preserves from suffering all those who respond to the divine direction – the centrality of the cross in his theology amply shows that. He meant that those who respond to this direction find that all experiences may be used to forward rather than thwart God's purposes. It is an affirmation of the ultimate redeemability of the world. On this understanding prayer is that activity by which we seek to identify ourselves with and bring ourselves into line with the pattern of God's attractive activity. Since the interiority of the world to God means that the responsiveness of a violin to a maestro is only a faint analogy of the responsiveness of all things to God then we may expect all sorts of 'miracles'. A 'miracle' on this understanding is not an 'intervention' or 'break' in the law of nature but rather the formation of a new pattern or harmony in response to God's direction. To vary the metaphor we can think of logs being floated down a river. At points these snag and jam; a 'miracle' is like the moment when a sudden eddy in the current unsnags the jam and brings all back into centre stream again. This account of miracles is not the event 'produced directly by God' but is not reductionist either. To say that no naturalistic explanation of a miracle could be complete is to say that both theological and spiritual factors have to be taken into account. The connection between miracles and 'faith' is that faith is the human quest to be caught into the stream of God's attractive direction. Matthew tells us that Jesus could do no 'mighty works' in his own country because of people's unbelief (Matt. 13.58). Unbelief is resistance to God's attraction, refusal to 'come into the stream'. Because God is gracious and free it is possible to make this refusal and this can effectively preclude 'miracles'. The Gethsemane prayer, 'not what I will but what you will', is not a semi-believing caveat to prayers of intercession but rather the recognition that providence is directed by Wisdom, and that there are many things which may seem attractive or desirable to us which would contravene that Wisdom. We can pray then, as Jesus did in Gethsemane, with all the passion at our disposal. But prayer is, as Jesus' prayer was, a request to be caught up by the divine direction. Could this not have avoided tragedy? Why does crucifixion have to be part of it? The answer seems to be that if the universe is 'the arena of mankind's making above all other things' as Andrew Elphinstone puts it, then such an arena at once rules out compulsion and makes tragedy possible.[18]

It may be objected that this account of prayer, miracle, and the arena of human freedom does not take into account God's manner of acting in the incarnation and resurrection. How can these be understood as a new pattern or formation in response to the divine direction? This is how Schleiermacher wanted to understand them, as both 'miraculous' but at the same time integrated in the deepest way into the chain of cause and effect. Barth on the other hand refused to discuss them as miracles but spoke of them in terms of a new act of creation. They are not 'miracles' in the sense we have argued but rather the moments when God walks in amongst the actors in the most literal way. Together they also represent God's response to tragedy. On the cross we see the Wisdom of God crucified and dying alongside every other oppressed, tortured and murdered creature. Jesus' resurrection is the first fruits of the *new* creation, signifying God's refusal of our refusal, showing that we need not sorrow as 'those without hope'. It is the crucified and risen Christ who draws all humanity to himself: the transfigured beauty and the sign of ultimate hope. Like miracles both incarnation and resurrection indicate the *potential* of creation but unlike miracles they are not the result of a new pattern of existing events. What we have, rather, is the first moment of the new creation.

Can we pray for Northern Ireland?

Week by week churches throughout the world pray for trouble spots – divided communities where hatred and terror rule, like Northern Ireland, Sri Lanka, Lebanon, South Africa, El Salvador. For years nothing seems to happen. If anything it is attrition which rules. Does it make sense to go on praying for these situations? Does it make any difference? Does God actually 'direct' human history?

Langford offers a number of examples which might illustrate the way in which 'general' providence might be understood to influence history. The development of human cultures due to pressure on food resources or due to the development of science prompted by the human desire to know is an example. Another is the growth of social and economic conditions which provide the soil for the burst of genius we find, for example, in fourth-century Athens or fifteenth-century Florence. Such developments are more akin to the functioning of 'natural laws', and any deist can subscribe to such an account. If 'providence consists in action', however, then we will have to look elsewhere for God's providential direction of history.

A natural place to look is in the way great leaders have turned the destinies of nations in a liberating or life giving direction. 'How came we ashore?' asks Miranda in *The Tempest*, learning of her history. 'By Providence divine', Prospero replies, and so might we regard the incidents which, for instance, led Moses to demand Israel's release from slavery. In that case we are brought at once to the question of grace and human freedom (where 'grace' means, in the Augustinian sense, a direct divine influence on the human mind). It goes without saying that a God who directs by abandoning unlimited power cannot operate by brain washing. If we take the Moses story as a paradigm then we see first that Moses is led to his great role by a series of events which could receive a completely naturalistic explanation. Brought up in the house of Pharaoh his consciousness is first changed by seeing a Hebrew slave beaten by an Egyptian. An impetuous assault which ends in murder leads him to flee into the desert where he encounters the Kenites and their God YHWH. After a long period in that quite different culture (time to marry and have children), an encounter with YHWH sends him back to Egypt. This 'encounter' presupposes some kind or other of 'religious' experience, which is to say an experience of God, as a possibility for human beings. Without subscribing to any theory of mysticism we may believe that prayer may often be involved in such experiences, at least as a way of putting us in the way of them. What is important here, where the question of how God respects creaturely freedom is at issue, is that the experience is of a command which is an invitation at the same time. It can be disobeyed or refused, and the story actually records many hesitations on Moses' part. Langford speculates that God's providence may have to reckon with many instances of refusal, as well as acceptances of the divine invitation.[19] Part of reckoning with the true humanity of Jesus will be that he too was called and could have turned down his call – even this was not precluded by incarnation. By analogy with this story, if we are praying for Northern Ireland or wherever it may be, we are praying for those individuals who, at great cost to themselves, seek to lead people into a situation which is more life-giving, a situation like that achieved by the Judges of Israel, characterized by 'shalom', peace and justice.

Beyond this, talk of providence in history is necessarily a matter of interpretation. For Calvin's 'providence consists in action' we could equally say, 'providence consists in interpretation'. In *The Embarrassment of Riches*, an account of the golden age of Dutch history, Simon Schama records how an entire culture interpreted its history, down to the smallest detail, in terms of providence. The concept functioned as a way in which a newly liberated but religiously pluralist community could understand its identity. 'Every Sunday (at least) a cascade of rhetoric would crash down from the pulpit, invoking the destiny of the Hebrews as though the congregation were itself a tribe of Israel. Lines dividing history and scripture dissolved as the meaning of Dutch independence and power was attributed to the providential selection of a new people to be as a light unto the nations.'[20] Both the history of the Dutch settlers in Southern Africa and the sense of Prussian destiny which we find equally in Hegel and Bismarck, and which was one of the many factors which contributed to the Holocaust, remind us of the dangers of reading history as providence. Yet the process Schama details so vividly also provides a model for both individual and community. If God is really active in the world, and if we can put ourselves in the way of that action, then we have no option but to look for the guidance of his hand. To do this we need rules of interpretation, and these are provided, as the Calvinist preachers maintained, in scripture. Like the Calvinists a present day liberation theologian, Leonardo Boff, can speak of salvation and the kingdom of God being realized in freedom movements 'because everything is open to and penetrated by the ultimate will of God'.[21] This is effectively a claim to discern God's providence which, like that in seventeenth-century Holland (where the struggle against Spain was understood in terms of Israel in Egypt), rests on the discernment of the centrality of the question of human freedom in scripture. Using scripture in this way is what gives content to the claim that it is 'inspired'. Claims for scriptural inspiration, or talk of the scriptural 'canon', are in effect ways of ascribing normative significance to the way of interpreting history we find in these documents.

John Barton has pointed out that claims like these are implicit in the famous bidding prayer of the King's College Carol Service, which invites us to 'trace the loving purposes of God' from our first disobedience to redemption in Christ.[22] He is critical of these claims, failing to respect as they do the fact that the biblical narrative is 'history like' rather than history proper. He believes we are faced with a sharp alternative: either we must try to detect God's providence in the whole of history, or we can allow the biblical narrative to function as the horizon of thought. We cannot do both. Attempts to combine the two in the liturgy, moving from an evolutionary account of creation to biblical salvation history, represent 'an impossible mingling of two idioms of thought'. Because theology is not an esoteric game but a set of assertions about how things really are we must take the former option, abandon sacred history and speak the language of evolution. The question we need to ask is not the intra-textual one of how the Christian story fits in to that of Israel, but what can be said about Jesus in the context of human history and human religious thought.

The problem here is how these two options are to be distinguished – the way in which 'Old' and 'New' Testaments fit together is a crucial part of 'human history and human religious thought'. In the same way the story of evolution and the story of Abraham and Moses are not simply 'incommensurable'. From the perspective of faith evolution is the story of the arrival of homo sapiens on the scene; human history represents evolution on another level; the story of Abraham and his successors is one extraordinarily fertile way of making sense of that continuing evolution. So-called 'sacred story' is simply part of the whole story which, for various reasons (say, the resurrection of Jesus), we invest with decisive hermeneutic significance for understanding all events, including those spoken of by cosmologists. Buddhists might say the same for the story of Gautama, and Muslims (perhaps more problematically) for Muhammed. 'Second naivete' is not required to do this. No science whatever establishes its own horizon; all work within cultural horizons of which various sacred stories form a part.

If we accept that the biblical story may give us a clue to the interpretation of history in general then we can also ascribe hermeneutic significance to two other histories – those of Israel and church. Famously it was the history of the Jews which Frederick the Great's physician offered him as a 'proof' of God's existence. Driven into the nations, harried, scattered and persecuted, we can nevertheless claim that God's providence can be discerned here, if we begin from scripture.

In the same way God's providence is the account of how the story of the crucified Jew Jesus bears on human history. It is, in other words, the *history* of the atonement. The 'atonement' is not something which happened only on Calvary; it is Calvary made real in human history through the Holy Spirit. As R. C. Moberly put it classically at the beginning of the century, the atonement was objective that it might become subjective in repentance, faith and love.[23] When we ask what 'Spirit' means here we need to go on, like Moberly, to speak of church and sacraments. Christian mission is a question of telling the story of Jesus which is redemptive as it constitutes an invitation to turn away from the idols of greed, self-aggrandisement, and the use of force they rely on ('Mammon' or, alternatively, social Darwinism) to the living God whose power is that of vicarious love. The story is an *invitation* to see and to structure life differently. This invitation gives rise to community. We are as we are in relation and we change, become renewed or different people, as we are called into a community which seeks to live by the redeeming story. This is not to opt for a reductionist account of 'Spirit', equating it with the 'common spirit' as Schleiermacher did. It is to say that the Spirit works, as God always works, in ways which can be given completely naturalistic explanations. It is also to say that the 'personal relationship with Jesus' which accounts for our change or renewal is mediated by the community. Through this story-telling people are changed, and thus history is changed (for 'history' is not an abstraction which God can direct but consists of movements and individuals with whom God engages).

Both stories are about the power of weakness. Both affirm that whilst history seems to be an account of the great and powerful, the pursuit of power and gain in fact run counter to the innermost rationale of creation, the divine Wisdom. Both stories speak of God's action in and through the lives of human communities, full of sin and error as they are. Jesus' story insists that when the Jewish faith is true to itself it is about the God who works through the Suffering Servant, through forgiveness and through 'being for others', vicariousness. These stories detail the 'weakness' which is power, and they offer the only certain clue to God's constant working. They make the point that 'providence' cannot necessarily be discerned in the victory or success of the righteous. If we ask again how this bears on the question of whether we pray for Northern Ireland, then what we are bidden to do is to *discern* where God is at work, according to these criteria, and to pray accordingly.[24]

Another example of this mode of God's direction might be the history of the canon, as Barth suggested. The length of time this took and the uncertainties which attended the process, are often felt to count against recognizing divine direction in the formation of the canon. But from the point of view of an attractive providence length of time and uncertainty are exactly what we would expect. We can discern God's rule in the way that some books slowly commended themselves to the community whilst others, at first generally accepted, slowly receded in importance. We discern a rule through attraction in the very fact that the canon remains open so that what is authoritative and normative remains open to discussion. At the same time in and through this discussion God's rule is exercised as certainly as it was in the defeat of Achitophel's counsel by Hushai or in the story-telling of Nathan. We can also see in the canon the variety of the means of God's direction. It is conceived now in terms of the beauty of worship, now in terms of Wisdom, now in terms of the Suffering Servant. This 'direction' is gracious because it is not the book which fell from heaven, which calls to be interpreted univocally in every situation, but because in it the Word of God speaks through historical community to historical community. It 'directs' us by its intrinsic authority and the attraction of truth, and not through the compulsion of any Propaganda Office.

Is belief in providence compatible with belief in progress? Providence in history, we can say, is essentially about the fulfilment of the prayer that God's kingdom come on earth, as in heaven. In his life and teaching Jesus spelled out what the values of the kingdom were and to talk of 'progress' is to claim that we can discern these values being realized for instance in the womens' rights or human rights movements. It is ironical that someone like Augustine, who had the highest faith in providence, had at the same time little faith in what we would call progress, a position which has no lack of twentieth-century supporters (Reinhold Niebuhr for example). There seems, however, to be an out and out contradiction between the claim that providence consists in action and the claim that this action produces no discernible results in the long run. Far from being incompatible with progress belief in providence seems actually to require it.

The question is sometimes raised whether a God who directs or rules in this way, through weakness, through the crucified Jesus, through Israel and through the church, really commands our worship. The question is much rather whether any other concept of God could do so. Here once for all we see that we do not have to do with any 'Almighty Tyrant' and that God's true sovereignty, God's own confidence in the power of love, is known through his entrusting himself to the historical process in this way.

Faith in providence is, then, a matter of a particular *pattern* of discernment. It is confidence in the ultimate rationality of God's Wisdom as expressed in the cross. We discern there both a divine refusal of hatred and violence and also the proclamation of the divine bias in history. We are not offered a paternalist god who constantly puts everything right for us but a God who is alongside the oppressed in their darkness, poverty and despair. The cross is the heart of providence. Here, where the Son of Man cannot come down from the cross, we see what it means that providence consists in action. Here we see the guidance of creation to its proper end, God's loving and wise care for the creature. Providence is the attractive and endlessly engaging initiative of a love which cannot be deterred, which we encounter in our lives, fashioning us often against what seems to be the grain, and fashioning human history in the same way. It is the gracious God in action.

Postscript

Can God be Defeated?

Understanding providence in terms of an elicitation of the creature's creativity we have been led to affirm the freedom of response of the whole created order, what the tradition has polemically called 'autonomy'. God's direction is gracious, an offer, an invitation, a wooing, and invitations and allurements can be refused. The immediate answer to the question' 'Can God be defeated?' would seem to be that of course he is 'defeated' all the time in that sin and evil represent the refusal of his allurement. Yet what the Old Testament writers call God's *ḥesed*, his loving kindness or solidarity with the creature, represents his refusal of our refusal, the refusal to accept defeat. But could there be something – say the destruction of the world in a nuclear holocaust – which represented an *ultimate* defeat of God, such that the labour of evolution was shown to be unjustified, such that the attractiveness of grace was seen not to have succeeded because the end product was a creature too flawed to realize God's purposes?

Those who reflected in Israel wrestled with something like this problem as they tried to understand their people's recurrent failure to live according to what they saw to be YHWH's revealed will. Naturally their response was diverse and included many readings of God's presence to history and of the eschatological hope engendered by present distress and failure. In the light of the cross the church (whether in the New Testament period or later is really immaterial) fixed especially on the figure of the

Servant of Isaiah 53 where *it is precisely in defeat that God is victorious*. What the tradition has taken from this, however, is not a glorying in defeat for its own sake but rather the insight that it is the ability to turn utter defeat – malice, hatred, destruction, refusal – into victory which is what makes God God. But how, then, is this related to eschatology, the 'last things'? If the Jewish and Christian account of creation from nothing be true then we live in a finite, not an infinitely cyclical, world. Certainly all accounts of the future of this universe offered by the natural sciences include the end of the present order as we know it. From the Christian point of view this only confirms traditional eschatological language which thinks of this order as ultimate in significance, because the Son of Man is at the centre of it, but provisional in time. In other words, the tradition has not understood the certain end of this world order to mean defeat for God but rather as ushering in the consummation of his purpose. This does not mean, however, as fundamentalist groups in America have understood it, that a nuclear holocaust is just what we need to bring in the kingdom and fulfil God's purposes. This kind of thinking, and that act, were it ever to be realized, would certainly constitute the ultimate in what appears to be God's long running series of defeats, a supreme Johannine irony in which the pious would again crucify the incarnation of God's purpose. Would such a defeat, however, as the end of human history, be irredeemable? Would it be more irredeemable, for instance, than Auschwitz? God turns defeat, according to the insight expressed on the cross, by bearing the world's pain, guilt, refusal and sin himself, and by forgiving it.

There are two questions, then, which need to be asked to decide whether there is anything finally irredeemable. In the first place, it is *God* who turns defeat. There is a question whether the destruction of the creation would mean the death of the Creator, as Dorothee Sölle has proposed.[1] Against this possibility Moltmann appeals to a 'protest theism' which insists that the murderer cannot triumph over the victim. Belief in the eternity of God, here God's absolute freedom *vis à vis* creation, is not a superficial hope for 'pie in the sky' but rather an affirmation of faith in the non-absurdity of all things. 'Protest theism' and the 'protest atheism' of Ivan Karamazov or, for that matter, J. S. Mill or Bertrand Russell, are complementary. 'Protest atheism rules out false religious consolation and irresponsible religious expedients. Protest theism sets possible crimes against humanity and all those who allow them by their passivity and indifference in the light of the divine judgement.'[2] On these grounds Rabbi Dan Cohn-Sherbok has insisted that belief in resurrection is the only possible theological response to the Holocaust. 'Without eventual vindication of the righteous in Paradise, there is no way to sustain the belief in a providential God who watches over his chosen people.'[3] Belief in the resurrection here is a form of 'protest theism' as it has frequently been over the centuries. In the same way any nuclear holocaust would call forth the 'protest of apocalyptic hope', as Moltmann puts it.[4]

The second question is whether there is anything which cannot finally be forgiven. Ivan Karamazov's answer is well known: if he had to share heaven with the man who had a child killed before his mother's eyes he would rather 'return the ticket'. The answer of Origen, on the other hand, later a victim of torture, was that even the devil would not be able ultimately to resist the attraction of God's love. Ironically it was Barth, the ferocious opponent of autonomy, who refused to go the whole way with this argument, maintaining that we could not rule out the possibility of a final refusal of God's purpose by some part of creation. If God is gracious, which is to say if he truly respects the creature, is Barth not right in this? Yet grace is that disposition which 'bears all things, believes all things, hopes all things, endures all things' (I Cor. 13.7). Such a disposition is only possible for the believer because it is first and pre-eminently true of God. It is God above all who bears, believes, hopes and endures all things. This means that belief in providence is not just, as Barth and Farmer describe it, faith in a 'Nevertheless'. It is the power of an unquenchable hope in the God of hope. Because God is gracious even he cannot presume on redemption, even he cannot be certain that refusal will not be final – but we hope in his hope. It is hope in that hope which is finally the only possible response to the question of whether God may be defeated. And it is hope in that hope which leads to the great affirmation of Paul:

> I am sure that neither death, nor life, nor angels, nor principalities, nor things present, nor things to come, nor powers, nor height, nor depth, nor anything else in all creation, will be able to separate us from the love of God in Christ Jesus our Lord (Rom. 8.38-9).

NOTES

1. Disposing of False Friends

1. Hans Urs von Balthasar, *The Glory of the Lord*, Vol. VII, T. & T. Clark 1989, p. 134.

2. R. S. Thomas, 'The Island' in *Later Poems*, Macmillan 1983.

3. Ulrich Simon, *Pity and Terror*, Macmillan 1989, p. x.

4. F. D. E. Schleiermacher, *The Christian Faith*, T. & T. Clark 1928, p. 725.

5. Karl Barth, *Church Dogmatics* III/3, T. & T. Clark 1960, p. 33.

6. John Calvin, *Institutes of the Christian Religion*, 1.16.3.

7. In the Hensley Henson Lectures for 1990; not yet published.

8. Thomas Aquinas, *Summa Theologiae*, 1a.23.1.

9. *Summa*, 1a.22.3.

10. Calvin, *Institutes*, 1.16.4.

11. Ibid., 1.17.13.

12. Ibid., 1.18.2.

13 Barth, *Church Dogmatics* III/3, p.3.

14. Augustine, *De Civitate Dei*, 5.9.

15. *Summa*, 1a.116.3.

16. Former President Reagan is said to have consulted horoscopes before making important decisions.

17. Cf. Max Weber's remark that 'so long and insofar as the *Karma* doctrine remained unshaken, revolutionary ideas or the striving for "progress" were inconceivable', in *The Religion of India*, Glencoe 1958, p. 123.

18. D. J. Bartholomew, *God of Chance*, SCM Press 1984.

19. Karl Barth, *Church Dogmatics* II/2, 1957, p.50.

20. Calvin, *Institutes*, 1.16.8; 17.11.

21. J. Monod, *Chance and Necessity*, Collins 1972.

22. W. G. Pollard, *Chance and Providence*, Scribner 1958, p.180.

23. Bartholomew, *God of Chance* (n. 18).

24. Ibid., p. 98.

25. M. F. Wiles, *God's Action in the World*, SCM Press 1986, p. 103.

26. Aquinas, *Summa*, 1a.45.6.

27. Ibid., 1a.104.1.

28. Schleiermacher, *Christian Faith* (n.4), p. 143.

29. P. Tillich, *Systematic Theology*, SCM Press 1968, vol. 1, p.296.

30. I. Barbour, *Issues in Science and Religion*, SCM Press and Harper & Row 1966, p. 385.

31. T. F. Torrance, *Divine and Contingent Order*, Oxford University Press 1981, p. 30.

32. Barbour, *Issues* (n.30), p.269.

2. Can We Do Theology by Doing Science?

1. J. Polkinghorne, *Science and Creation*, SPCK 1988.

2. Karl Barth, *Church Dogmatics* I/1, T. & T. Clark 1936, p. 7.

3. *Church Dogmatics* III/1, 1958, p. x.

4. Torrance's arguments can be found in a whole string of publications chief amongst which are *Theological Science*, Oxford University Press 1969; *Space, Time and Incarnation*, Oxford University Press 1969; *God and Rationality*, Oxford University Press 1971; *Theology in Reconciliation*, Oxford University Press 1975; *Space, Time and Resurrection*, Scottish Academic Press 1976; *Divine and Contingent Order*, Oxford University Press 1981. Cf. John Polkinghorne, *One World*, SPCK 1987; *Science and Creation*, SPCK 1988; *Science and Providence*, SPCK 1989.

5. Polkinghorne, *One World*, p. 25.

6. In *Theology and the Philosophy of Science*, Darton, Longman & Todd 1976.

7. Ibid., p. 273.

8. Ibid., p. 303.

9. Ibid., p. 341.

10. *Space, Time and Resurrection* (n.4), p. ix. Torrance knows better than anybody that Barth used the term 'natural theology' to cover a multitude of sins, from Kantian moralism to Bultmannian existentialism, as well as the classical arguments of Anselm and Aquinas.

11. Polkinghorne, *Science and Creation* (n. 4), p. 6.

12. Ibid., p. 73.

13. Polkinghorne, *One World*, p. 80.

14. Ibid., p. 78.

15. Torrance, *Space, Time and Resurrection*, p. 180.

16. Polkinghorne, *One World*, p. 64.

17. P. Fiddes, *The Creative Suffering of God*, Oxford University Press 1988, p. 39.

18. D.J. Bartholomew, *God of Chance*, SCM Press 1984, pp. 55-56; Bartholomew's italics.

19. Ibid., p. 63.

20. Torrance, *Divine and Contingent Order* (n.4), p. 66.

21. H. McCabe, *God Matters*, Chapman 1987, p. 58.

22. Torrance, *Space, Time and Incarnation (n.4), pp. 71, 76*.

23. *Space, Time and Resurrection*, p. 90.

24. J. Moltmann, *God in Creation*, SCM Press and Harper & Row 1985, pp. 86-87.

25. Polkinghorne, *One World*, p. 64.

26. Barth, *Church Dogmatics* I/1, pp. 8-9.

27. Polkinghorne, *Science and Creation*, p. 97; Einstein's original statement was: 'Religion without science is blind, science without religion is lame.'

28. *Space, Time and Incarnation*, p. 69.

29. Aquinas, *Summa Theologiae*, 1a.14.8.

30. *Summa*, 1a.22.1.

31. Ibid., 1a.105.5.

32. B. Russell, *Mysticism and Logic*, Allen & Unwin 1919, p. 180.

33. David Hume, *A Treatise of Human Nature*, ed. Selby Bigge, Oxford University Press 1988, p. 225.

34. *Summa* 1a.19.8.

35. Ibid., 1a.22.4.

36. Ibid., 1a.14.13.

37. T. Gilby in vol. 5 of the New Blackfriars edition of *Summa Theologiae*, Eyre & Spottiswood 1964, p. 103. In the *Summa Contra Gentes* Aquinas appears to give a place to luck or chance in events (Book 3 ch.74), but he argues for this on the same grounds as his argument for contingent events and the same objection applies.

38. David Hume, *Enquiries concerning the Human Understanding*, ed. Selby Bigge, Oxford University Press 1902, p. 103.

39. *Church Dogmatics* III/3, 1960, p. 100.

40. McCabe has now gone back on this expression, which I continue to find helpful. Cf. *God Matters* (n.21), p. 1.

41. Cf. M. Langford, *Providence*, SCM Press 1981, pp. 32f.

3. Providence and Evil

1. J. S. Mill, *Three Essays in Religion*, 1874, pp. 186-87.

2. *Church Dogmatics* III/3, p. 300.

3. Karl Barth, *How I Changed My Mind*, T. & T. Clark 1969, p. 86.

4. J. Hick, *Evil and the God of Love*, Macmillan 1966, pp. 214-15.

5. H.H. Farmer, *The World and God*, Nisbet 1935, p. 215.

6. Ibid., p. 233.

7. A. Elphinstone, *Freedom, Suffering and Love*, SCM Press 1976, p. 55.

8. Ibid., pp. 56-7.

9. P. Fiddes, *The Creative Suffering of God*, Oxford University Press 1988, pp. 228-29.

10. Bartholomew, *God of Chance*, p. 109.

11. G. von Rad, *Genesis*, SCM Press and Westminster Press 1963, p. 87.

12. F. D. E. Schleiermacher, *The Christian Faith*, T. & T. Clark 1928, p. 273.

13. Ibid., p. 328.

14. J. L. Segundo, *Evolution and Guilt*, Gill & Macmillan and Orbis Books 1973, p. 9.

15. In James Hastings, *Encyclopaedia of Religion and Ethics*, T. & T. Clark 1908ff, vol. 11, p. 542.

16. Segundo, op. cit., p. 84.

17. Ibid., p. 129.

18. Augustine, *De Civitate Dei*, 12.6-7.

19. Ibid., 14.3.
20. Hick, op. cit (n.4), p. 150.
21. *Church Dogmatics* III/3, p. 352.
22. Hick, op. cit., p. 145.
23. J. Cowburn, *Shadows and the Dark*, SCM Press 1979, p. 58.
24. E. Brunner, *The Mediator*, Lutterworth 1934, p. 124.
25. In *New Essays in Philosophical Theology*, ed. A. Flew and A. MacIntyre, SCM Press 1955, pp. 144f.

4. Knowledge, Power and Providence

1. B. Russell, *The Scientific Outlook*, Allen & Unwin 1949, pp. 130f.
2. Cf. *De Trinitate* XV, 22; Aquinas, *Summa Theologiae*, 1a.14.
3. *De Trinitate* XV, 2.
4. *De Civitate Dei*, 11.21.
5. Boethius, *De Consolatione Philosophiae*, 5.4.
6. *De Praedestinatione Sanctorum*, 19.
7. Aquinas, *Summa*, 1a.25.
8. Karl Barth, *Church Dogmatics* III/3. p. 131.
9. Cf. *Church Dogmatics* II/1, p. 557; Barth, *Dogmatics in Outline*, SCM Press 1949, p. 123.
10. *Church Dogmatics* III/3, p. 150.
11. Ibid., p. 289 my italics.
12. Ibid., p. 556.
13. *Church Dogmatics* II/1, p. 580.
14. Ibid. p. 578.
15. H. H. Farmer, *The World and God*, Nisbet 1935, p. 211.
16. W. Eichrodt, *Old Testament Theology*, vol. 1, SCM Press and Harper & Row 1967, p. 179.
17. L. Köhler, *Old Testament Theology*, Fortress Press 1958, p. 35.
18. C. Raven, *War and the Christian*, SCM Press 1938, p. 51.
19. D. Bonhoeffer, *Letters and Papers from Prison*, SCM Press, revised and enlarged edition 1971, pp. 360-61.
20. *Church Dogmatics*, IV/1, p. 186.
21. H. McCabe, *God Matters*, Chapman 1987, pp. 39f.
22. P. Fiddes, *The Creative Suffering of God*, ch. 1.
23. Ibid., p. 39.
24. McCabe, op. cit., p. 74.
25. Fiddes, op. cit., p. 91.
26. *Church Dogmatics*, II/1, p. 613.
27. J. Moltmann, *The Trinity and the Kingdom of God*, SCM Press 1981 (= *Trinity and the Kingdom*, Harper & Row 1981), pp. 124f.
28. Fiddes, op. cit., p. 164.
29. G. Gutiérrez, *The Power of the Poor in History*, SCM Press and Orbis Books 1983.

5. Divine Direction

1. Karl Barth, *Church Dogmatics* III/3, p. 139.
2. Aquinas, *Summa Theologiae*, 1a.13.5.

3. P. Sherry, 'Analogy Today' in *Philosophy* 51, 1976, pp. 431f.

4. J. M. Soskice, *Metaphor and Religious Language*, Oxford University Press 1985, p. 15.

5. Ibid., p. 115. Soskice distinguishes analogies from metaphors by the greater appropriateness of the former. Metaphors involve more 'imaginative strain' and thus have a greater power to generate new perspectives; pp. 65-66.

6. Ibid., p. 124.

7. Ibid., p. 115.

8. Aquinas, *Summa*, 1a.2ae.91.

9. *Church Dogmatics* IV/1, p. 187.

10. M. Langford, *Providence*, SCM Press 1981, p. 5.

11. See above p. ix.

12. *Church Dogmatics* II/1, p. 661.

13. The phrase is Robert Jenson's, on whose illuminating discussion I draw in the next two paragraphs; cf. R. Jenson, *The Triune Identity*, Fortress Press 1982.

14. P. Brook, *The Empty Space*, 1968, Penguin edition 1972.

15. W. Sherlock, *Discourse Concerning Divine Providence*, 1694, cited in Langford, op. cit (n.10), p. 90.

16. Brook, *The Empty Space*, p. 43.

17. Ibid., p. 120.

18. D. Selbourne, *The Making of 'Midsummer Night's Dream'*, Methuen 1982, p. 21.

19. Fiddes, *The Creative Suffering of God*, p. 55.

20. Cf. P. Baelz, *Prayer and Providence*, SCM Press 1968, p. 66.

21. Brook, op. cit., p. 43.

22. Ibid., p. 138.

23. A. R. Peacocke, *Creation and the World of Science*, Oxford University Press 1979.

24. Brook op. cit., p. 55.

25. Ibid., pp. 56-7.

26. Ibid., p. 151.

27. Langford, op. cit., p. 135.

28. Aquinas, *Summa* 1a.105.5.

29. D. Bartholomew, *God of Chance*, SCM Press 1984, p. 140.

30. Langford, op. cit., p. 76.

6. For What Can We Pray?

1. J. Sobrino, *Christology at the Crossroads*, SCM Press and Orbis Books 1978, p. 147.

2. Ibid., p. 149.

3. Ibid.

4. Ibid., p. 157.

5. Ibid., p. 158.

6. H. Braun, *Jesus*, Stuttgart 1969, p.161; cited by Sobrino, ibid., p. 164.

7. Ibid., p. 175.

8. *Church Dogmatics* III/4, p. 93.

9. Ibid., p. 101.

10. Karl Barth, *Prayer and Preaching*, SCM Press 1964, p. 16.

11. *Church Dogmatics* III/4, p. 109.

12. M. F. Wiles, *God's Action in the World*, SCM Press 1986, p. 107.

13. H. H. Farmer, *The World and God*, Nisbet 1935, p. 166.

14. Ibid., p. 167.

15. *Church Dogmatics* III/4, p. 101.

16. Ibid., p. 100.

17. D. Bartholomew, *God of Chance*, p. 151.

18. A. Elphinstone, *Freedom, Suffering and Love*, SCM Press 1976, p. 4.

19. M. Langford, *Providence*, p. 126.

20. S. Schama, *The Embarrassment of Riches*, Fontana 1987, p. 94. For the same theme in general cf. pp. 45f., 94f., 114f., 119f.

21. L. Boff, *St Francis*, SCM Press and Crossroad Publishing 1985, p. 84.

22. John Barton, 'Preparation in History for Christ' in *The Religion of the Incarnation*, ed. R. Morgan, Bristol Classical Press 1989, p. 65.

23. R. C. Moberley, *Atonement and Personality*, John Murray 1907, p. 143.

24. In this connection the political prayers of most traditions, but particularly of the *Alternative Service Book*, need urgent revision. We cannot honestly go on praying as if we believe in the divine right of kings, and if we take the priority of the poor seriously, they should occupy the place in the litany currently occupied by prayers for the 'royal' family.

Postscript: Can God be Defeated?

1. D. Sölle, *To Work and To Love. A Theology of Creation*, Fortress 1984, pp. 209f.

2. J. Moltmann, *Creating a Just Future*, SCM Press and Trinity Press International 1989, p. 36.

3. D. Cohn-Sherbok, *Holocaust Theology*, Marshall Pickering 1989, p. 128.

4. Moltmann, op. cit., p. 38

INDEX